SUPPLEMENT ED

Areopagitica
freedom of the press

A Speech of Mr. John Milton
for the Liberty of Unlicensed Printing,
to the Parliament of England

LONDON,

PRINTED IN THE YEAR 1644

τοὐλεύθερον δ ἔκεινο · τίς θέλει πόλει
χρηστόν τι βούλευμ' ἐς μέσον φέρειν ἔχων
καὶ ταυθ ὁ χρῃζων λαμπρὸς ἔσθ', ὁ μὴ θέλων
σιγα · τί τούτων ἔστ ἰσαίτερον πόλει

This is true liberty, when freeborn men,
Having to advise the public, may speak freely,
And he who can and will, deserves high praise;
Who neither can nor will, may hold his peace;
What can be juster in a State than this?

Euripides —*The Suppliants*

BANDANNA BOOKS • 2011 • SANTA BARBARA

BANDANNA BOOKS COLLEGE TITLES

SAPPHO: THE POEMS.* Greece's greatest lyric poet. $9.95

AREOPAGITICA: FREEDOM OF THE PRESS.* John Milton.
Censorship history ancient and modern. $9.95

THE APOLOGY OF SOCRATES, & THE CRITO.* Plato. $9.95

THE FIRST DETECTIVE: THREE STORIES. EDGAR ALLAN POE.
    Poe's amateur detective Dupin was
    the model for Sherlock Holmes. $12.95

DON'T PANIC: THE PROCRASTINATOR'S GUIDE TO WRITING
    AN EFFECTIVE TERM PAPER. Steven Posusta. $11.95

MITOS Y LEYENDAS DE MÉXICO/MYTHS AND LEGENDS OF MEXICO.
    Luis Leal. Twenty origin stories and history.
    Color plates by Álvaro Ángel Suman. $39.50

GHAZALS OF GHALIB. Ghalib's witty couplets,
    arguing with God, his beloved. $9.95

THE MERCHANT OF VENICE. William Shakespeare. Art by
    Orson Welles. Edited by Rachel Burke. $11.95

GANDHI ON THE GITA. M.K. Gandhi explains the
    Bhagavad Gita chapter by chapter. $9.95

LEAVES OF GRASS, 1855 edition.*
    Walt Whitman. $11.95

ITALIAN FOR OPERA LOVERS. Italian opera terms. $5.95

DANTE & HIS CIRCLE. D. G. Rossetti. Italian love
    sonnets & Dante's *Vita Nuova*. $12.95

Order through our website at www.bandannabooks.com/bbooks
College Bookstores: fax orders for 5+ copies to 805-899-2145

*Teacher supplements available.

Contents

Editor's Note

Milton's essay on freedom of the press is one of the cornerstones of modern democracy. His survey of censorship shows the power of what was once known as a liberal education. John Milton was knowledgeable, thorough, yet driven by a passion for the life of the human spirit, and in the *Areopagitica*, he makes anew the case for freedom of the mind.

At the time of writing, Milton was young, a Latin poet. Recently back from a trip to Italy, he had met Galileo, then under house arrest by the Inquisition, who told him, in effective: "Don't let this happen in England." Milton's pamphlet (never actually given as a speech) endeavored to sway the Long Parliament away from continuing with a bureau of registry for printers and authors, the first step toward censorship. This work set the standard for freedom of the press.

Some phrases or words of uncommon usage are linked to endnotes. The two tasks of editing unique to this edition are modernization and gender choice. *Hath* must go, *unwillingest* becomes *most unwilling*.

What about gender? When Milton was writing in England, only boys went to school (or were elected to Parliament), so that his use of "he" as a "universal" pronoun seemed unobjectionable. For readers in our time, the text in this book is scheduled to be offered in ebook form in variant editions for third person singular personal pronouns.

Sasha Newborn, July 2011

AREOPAGITICA

They who to states and governors of the Commonwealth direct their speech, High Court of Parliament, or, wanting such access in a private condition, write that which they foresee may advance the public good; I suppose them, as at the beginning of no mean endeavor, not a little altered and moved inwardly in their minds—some with doubt of what will be the success, others with fear of what will be the censure; some with hope, others with confidence of what they have to speak. And me perhaps each of these dispositions, as the subject was whereon I entered, may have at other times variously affected; and likely might in these foremost expressions now also disclose which of them swayed most, but that the very attempt of this address thus made, and the thought of whom it has recourse to, has got the power within me to a passion far more welcome than incidental to a preface.

Which though I stay not to confess before any ask, I shall be blameless, if it be no other than the joy and gratulation which it brings to all who wish and promote their country's liberty; whereof this whole discourse proposed will be a certain testimony, if not a trophy. For this is not the liberty which we can hope, that no grievance ever should arise in the Commonwealth— that let no man in this world expect; but when complaints are freely heard, deeply considered, and speedily reformed, then is the utmost bound of civil liberty attained that wise men look for. To which, if I now manifest by the very sound of this which I shall utter, that we are already in good part arrived, and yet from such a steep disadvantage of tyranny and superstition grounded into our principles as was beyond the manhood of a Roman recovery; it will be attributed first, as is most due, to the strong assistance of God our deliverer, next, to your faithful guidance and undaunted wisdom, Lords and Commons of England. Neither is it in God's esteem the diminution of his glory, when honorable things are spoken of good people and worthy magistrates; which if I now first should begin to do, after so fair a progress of your laudable deeds and such a long obligement upon the whole realm to your indefatigable virtues, I might be justly reckoned among the tardiest and the most unwilling of them that praise you.

Nevertheless, there being three principal things without which all praising is but courtship and flattery: first, when that only is praised which is solidly worth praise; next, when greatest likelihoods are brought that such things are truly and really in those persons to whom they are ascribed; the other, when he who praises, by showing that such his actual persuasion is of whom he writes, can demonstrate that he flatters not; the former two of these I have heretofore endeavored, rescuing the employment from him who went about to impair your merits with a trivial and malignant encomium; the latter, as belonging chiefly to my own acquittal, that whom I so extolled I did not flatter, has been reserved opportunely to this occasion.

For he who freely magnifies what has been nobly done, and fears not to declare as freely what might be done better, gives you the best covenant of his fidelity; and that his loyalest affection and his hope waits on your proceedings. His highest praising is not flattery, and his plainest advice is a kind of praising; for though I should affirm and hold by argument that it would fare better with truth, with learning, and the Commonwealth, if one of your published orders, which I should name, were called in; yet at the same time it could not but much redound to the luster of your mild and equal government, whenas private persons are hereby animated to think you better pleased with public advice than other statists have been delighted heretofore with public flattery. And men will then see what difference there is between the magnanimity of a triennial Parliament, and that jealous haughtiness of prelates and cabin Counsellors that usurped of late, whenas they shall observe you in the midst of your victories and successes more gently brooking written exceptions against a voted order than other courts, which had produced nothing worth memory but the weak ostentation of wealth, would have endured the least signified dislike at any sudden proclamation.

If I should thus far presume upon the meek demeanor of your civil and gentle greatness, Lords and Commons, as what your published order has directly said, that to gainsay, I might defend myself with ease, if any should accuse me of being new or insolent, did they but know how much better I find you esteem it to imitate the old and elegant humanity of Greece, than the barbaric pride of a Hunnish and Norwegian stateliness. And out of those ages, to whose polite wisdom and letters we owe that we are not yet Goths and Jutlanders, I could name him [Isocrates] who from his private house wrote that discourse to the Parliament of Athens, that persuaded them to change the form of democracy which was then established. Such honor was done in those days to men who professed the study of wisdom and eloquence, not only in their own country but in other lands, that cities and seignories heard them gladly and with great respect, if they had anything in public to admonish the state. Thus did Dion Prusaeus [Chrysostomos], a stranger and a private orator, counsel the Rhodians against a former edict; and I abound with other like examples, which to set here would be superfluous.

But if from the industry of a life wholly dedicated to studious labors, and those natural endowments haply not the worst for two and fifty degrees of northern latitude, so much must be derogated, as to count me not equal to any of those who had this privilege, I would obtain to be thought not so inferior as yourselves are superior to the most of them who received their counsel: and how far you excel them, be assured, Lords and Commons, there can no greater testimony appear, than when your prudent spirit acknowledges and obeys the voice of reason from what quarter soever it be heard speaking, and renders you as willing to repeal any Act of your own setting forth, as any set forth by your predecessors.

If you be thus resolved, as it were injury to think you were not, I know not what should withhold me from presenting you with a fit instance wherein to show both that love of truth which you eminently profess, and that uprightness of your judgment which is not habitual to be partial to yourselves; by judging over again that Order which you have ordained to regulate printing: That no book, pamphlet, or paper shall be henceforth printed, unless the same be first approved and licensed by such, or at least one of such as shall be thereto appointed. For that part which preserves justly everyone's copy[right] to himself, or provides for the poor, I touch not, only wish they be not made pretenses to abuse and persecute honest and painful people, who offend not in either of these particulars. But that other clause of licensing books, which we thought had died with his brother quadragesimal and matrimonial when the prelates expired, I shall now attend with such a homily as shall lay before you, first, the inventors of it to be those whom you will be loath to own; next, what is to be thought in general of reading, whatever sort the books be; and that this Order avails nothing to the suppressing of scandalous, seditious, and libellous books, which were mainly intended to be suppressed. Last, that it will be primely to the discouragement of all learning, and the stop of truth, not only by disexercising and blunting our abilities in what we know already, but by hindering and cropping the discovery that might be yet further made both in religious and civil wisdom.

I deny not but that it is of greatest concernment in the Church. and Cornmonwealth to have a vigilant eye how books demean themselves as well as men; and thereafter to confine, imprison, and do sharpest justice on them as malefactors. For books are not absolutely dead things, but do contain a potency of life in them to be as active as that soul was whose progeny they are; nay, they do preserve as in a vial the purest efficacy and extraction of that living intellect that bred them. I know they are as lively, and as vigorously productive, as those fabulous dragon's teeth; and being sown up and down, may chance to spring up armed men. And yet, on the other hand, unless wariness be used, as good almost kill a man as kill a good book: who kills a man kills a reasonable creature, God's image; but he who destroys a good book, kills reason itself, kills the image of God, as it were, in the eye. Many a man lives a burden to the earth; but a good book is the precious life-blood of a master-spirit, embalmed and treasured up on purpose to a life beyond life. 'Tis true, no age can restore a life, whereof perhaps there is no great loss; and revolutions of ages do not often recover the loss of a rejected truth, for the lack of which whole nations fare the worse.

We should be wary, therefore, what persecution we raise against the living labors of public men, how we spill that seasoned life of humanity, preserved and stored up in books; since we see a kind of homicide may be thus committed, sometimes a martyrdom; and if it extend to the whole impression, a kind of massacre, whereof the execution ends not in the slaying of an elemental life, but strikes at that ethereal and fifth essence [quintessence], the breath of reason itself, slays an immortality rather than a life. But lest I should be condemned of introducing license, while I oppose licensing, I refuse not the pains to be so much historical as will serve to show what has been done by ancient and famous commonwealths against this disorder, till the very time that this project of licensing crept out of the Inquisition, was catched up by our prelates, and has caught some of our presbyters.

In Athens, where books and wits were ever busier than in any other part of Greece, I find but only two sorts of writings which the magistrates cared to take notice of; those either blasphemous and atheistical, or libellous. Thus the books of Protagoras were by the judges of Areopagus commanded to be burnt, and himself banished the territory for a discourse begun with his confessing not to know whether there were gods, or whether not. And against defaming, it was decreed that none should be traduced by name, as was the manner of vetus comoedia, whereby we may guess how they censured libelling; and this course was quick enough, as Cicero writes, to quell both the desperate wits of other atheists, and the open way of defaming, as the event showed. Of other sects and opinions, though tending to voluptuousness, and the denying of divine providence, they took no heed. Therefore we do not read that either Epicurus, or that libertine school of Cyrene, or what the Cynic impudence uttered, was ever questioned by the laws. Neither is it recorded that the writings of those old comedians were suppressed, though the acting of them were forbid; and that Plato commended the reading of Aristophanes, the loosest of them all, to his royal scholar Dionysius, is commonly known, and may be excused, if holy [John] Chrysostom as is reported, nightly studied so much the same author, and had the art to cleanse a scurrilous vehemence into the style of a rousing sermon.

That other leading city of Greece, Lacedaemon, con- sidering that Lycurgus their lawgiver was so addicted to elegant learning as to have been the first that brought out of Ionia the scattered works of Homer, and sent the poet Thales from Crete to prepare and mollify the Spartan surliness with his smooth songs and odes, the better to plant among them law and civility, it is to be wondered how museless and unbookish they were, minding nothing but the feats of war. There needed no licensing of books among them, for they disliked all but their own laconic apothegms, and took a slight occasion to chase Archilochus out of their city, perhaps for composing in a higher strain than their own soldierly ballads and roundels could reach to; or if it were for his broad verses, they were not therein so cautious, but they were as dissolute in their promiscuous conversing; whence Euripides affirms in Andromache, that their women were all unchaste. Thus much may give us light after what sort of books were prohibited among the Greeks.

The Romans also, for many ages trained up only to a military roughness, resembling most the Lacedaemonian guise, knew of learning little but what their Twelve Tables, and the Pontific College with their augurs and flamens taught them in religion and law, so unacquainted with other learning, that when Carneades and Critolaus, with the Stoic Diogenes coming ambassadors to Rome, took thereby occasion to give the city a taste of their philosophy, they were suspected for seducers by no less a person than Cato the Censor, who moved it in the Senate to dismiss them speedily, and to banish all such Attic babblers out of Italy. But Scipio and others of the noblest senators withstood him and his old Sabine austerity; honored and admired the men; and the Censor himself at last, in his old age, fell to the study of that whereof before he was so scrupulous. And yet at the same time, Naevius and Plautus, the first Latin comedians, had filled the city with all the borrowed scenes of Menander and Philemon.

Then began to be considered there also what was to be done to libellous books and authors; for Naevius was quickly cast into prison for his unbridled pen, and released by the tribunes upon his recantation; we read also that libels were burnt, and the makers punished by Augustus. The like severity, no doubt, was used, if anything were impiously written against their esteemed gods. Except in these two points, how the world went in books, the magistrate kept no reckoning. And therefore Lucretius without impeachment versifies his Epicurism to Memmius, and had the honor to be set forth the second time by Cicero, so great a father of the commonwealth; although himself disputes against that opinion in his own writings. Nor was the satirical sharpness or naked plainness of Lucilius, or Catullus, or Flaccus [Quintus Horatius Flaccus, Horace] by any order prohibited.

And for matters of state, the story of Titus Livius [Livy], though it extolled that part which Pompey held, was not therefore suppressed by Octavius Caesar of the other faction. But that Naso [Publius Ovidius Naso, Ovid] was by him banished in his old age for the wanton poems of his youth, was but a mere covert of state over some secret cause: and besides, the books were neither banished nor called in. From hence we shall meet with little else but tyranny in the Roman Empire, that we may not marvel, if not so often bad as good books were silenced. I shall therefore deem to have been large enough in producing what among the ancients was punishable to write, save only which, all other arguments were free to treat on.

By this time the emperors were become Christians, whose discipline in this point I do not find to have been more severe than what was formerly in practice. The books of those whom they took to be grand heretics were examined, refuted, and condemned in the general councils; and not till then were prohibited, or burnt, by authority of the emperor. As for the writings of heathen authors, unless they were plain invectives against Christianity, as those of Porphyrius and Proclus, they met with no interdict that can be cited, till about the year 400, in a Carthaginian Council, wherein bishops themselves were forbid to read the books of Gentiles, but heresies they might read: while others long before them, on the contrary, scrupled more the books of heretics than of Gentiles. And that the primitive councils and bishops were inclined only to declare what books were not commendable, passing no further, but leaving it to each one's conscience to read or to lay by, till after the year 800, is observed already by Padre Paolo [Pietro Sarpi], the great unmasker of the Trentine Council.

After which time the Popes of Rome, engrossing what they pleased of political rule into their own hands, extended their dominion over people's eyes, as they had before over their judgments, burning and prohibiting to be read what they fancied not; yet sparing in their censures, and the books not many which they so dealt with; till Martin V, by his Bull, not only prohibited, but was the first that excommunicated the reading of heretical books; for about that time Wyclif and Huss growing terrible, were they who first drove the Papal Court to a stricter policy of prohibiting. Which course Leo X and his successors followed, until the Council of Trent and the Spanish Inquisition, engendering together, brought forth, or perfected those catalogues, and expurging indexes, that rake through the entrails of many an old good author, with a violation worse than any could be offered to his tomb.

Nor did they stay in matters heretical, but any subject that was not to their palate, they either condemned in a prohibition, or had it straight into the new purgatory of an Index. To fill up the measure of encroachment, their last invention was to ordain that no book, pamphlet, or paper should be printed (as if St. Peter had bequeathed them the keys of the press also out of Paradise) unless it were approved and licensed under the hands of two or three glutton friars. For example:

Let the Chancellor Cini be pleased to see if in this present work be contained anything that may withstand the printing.

Vincent Rabbatta, Vicar of Florence.

I have seen this present work, and find nothing athwart the Catholic faith and good manners: in witness whereof I have given,

&c.   Nicolò Cini, Chancellor of Florence.

Attending the precedent relation, it is allowed that this present work of Davanzati may be printed.

Vincent Rabatta, Vicar of Florence.

It may be Printed, July 15.

Friar Simon Mompei d'Amelia,

Chancellor of the holy office in Florence.

Sure they have a conceit, if he of the bottomless pit had not long since broke prison, that this quadruple exorcism would bar him down. I fear their next design will be to get into their custody the licensing of that which they say Claudius intended, but went not through with [Quo veniem daret flatum crepitumque ventris in convivio emittendi—Suetonius]. Vouchsafe to see another of their forms, the Roman stamp:

Imprimatur, If it seem good to the reverend Master of the Holy Palace, ...

Belcastro, Viceregent.

Imprimatur,

> Friar Nicolò Rodolphi, Master of the Holy Palace.

Sometimes five Imprimaturs [Latin for "It may be printed") are seen together, dialoguewise, in the piazza of one title-page, complimenting and ducking each to other with their shaven reverences, whether the author, who stands by in perplexity at the foot of his epistle, shall to the press or to the sponge [expunged]. These are the pretty responsories, these are the dear antiphonies that so bewitched of late our prelates and their chaplains with the goodly echo they made; and besotted us to the gay imitation of a lordly Imprimatur, one from Lambeth House [residence of the Archbishop of Canterbury], another from the west end of [St.] Paul's [headquarters of the Bishop of London], so apishly romanizing that the word of command still was set down in Latin; as if the learned grammatical pen that wrote it would cast no ink without Latin; or perhaps, as they thought, because no vulgar tongue was worthy to express the pure conceit of an Imprimatur; but rather, as I hope, for that our English, the language of people ever famous and foremost in the achievements of liberty, will not easily find servile letters enough to spell such a dictatory presumption English.

And thus you have the inventors and the original of book-licensing ripped up and drawn as lineally as any pedigree. We have it not, that can be heard of, from any ancient state, or polity, or church, nor by any statute left us by our ancestors elder or later; nor from the modern custom of any reformed city or church abroad; but from the most anti-christian council and the most tyrannous inquisition that ever inquired. Till then books were ever as freely admitted into the world as any other birth; the issue of the brain was no more stifled than the issue of the womb; no envious Juno sat cross-legged over the nativity of any man's intellectual offspring; but if it proved a monster, who denies but that it was justly burnt, or sunk into the sea. But that a book, in worse condition than a peccant soul, should be to stand before a jury before it be born to the world, and undergo yet in darkness the judgment of Radamanth and his colleagues, before it can pass the ferry backward into light, was never heard before, till that mysterious iniquity, provoked and troubled at the first entrance of Reformation, sought out new limbos and new hells wherein they might include our books also within the number of their damned. And this was the rare morsel so officiously snatched up, and so ill-favoredly imitated by our inquisiturient bishops, and the attendant minorites, their chaplains. That you like not now these most certain authors of this licensing order, and that all sinister intention was far distant from your thoughts, when you were importuned the passing it, all people know the integrity of your actions, and how you honor truth, will clear you readily.

But some will say, what though the inventors were bad, the thing for all that may be good. It may so; yet if that thing be no such deep invention, but obvious and easy for any man to light on, and yet best and wisest commonwealths through all ages and occasions have forborne to use it, and falsest seducers and oppressors of man were the first who took it up, and to no other purpose but to obstruct and hinder the first approach of Reformation; I am of those who believe it will be a harder alchemy than Lullius [Raymond Lully] ever knew to sublimate any good use out of such an invention. Yet this only is what I request to gain from this reason, that it may be held a dangerous and suspicious fruit, as certainly it deserves, for the tree that bore it, until I can dissect one by one the properties it has. But I have first to finish, as was propounded, what is to be thought in general of reading books, whatever sort they be, and whether be more the benefit or the harm that thence proceeds?

Not to insist upon the examples of Moses, Daniel, and Paul, who were skilful in all the learning of the Egyptians, Chaldeans, and Greeks, which could not probably be without reading their books of all sorts; in Paul especially, who thought it no defilement to insert into holy Scripture the sentences of three Greek poets, and one of them a tragedian; the question was notwithstanding sometimes controverted among the primitive doctors, but with great odds on that side which affirmed it both lawful and profitable, as was then evidently perceived when Julian the Apostate and subtlest enemy to our faith, made a decree forbidding Christians the study of heathen learning; for, said he, they wound us with our own weapons, and with our own arts and sciences they overcome us. And, indeed, the Christians were put so to their shifts by this crafty means, and so much in danger to decline into all ignorance, that the two Apollinarii were compelled, as a person may say, to coin all the seven liberal sciences out of the Bible, reducing it to diverse forms of orations, poems, dialogues, even to the calculating of a new Christian grammar. But, says the historian Socrates [Scholasticus], the providence of God provided better than the industry of Apollinarius and his son, by taking away that illiterate law with the life of him who devised it.

So great an injury they then held it to be deprived of Hellenic learning; and thought it a persecution more undermining, and secretly decaying the Church, than the open cruelty of Decius or Diocletian. And perhaps it was the same politic drift that the devil whipped St. Jerome in a Lenten dream for reading Cicero; or else it was a phantasm bred by the fever which had then seized him. For had an angel been his discipliner, unless it were for dwelling too much upon Ciceronianisms, and had chastised the reading, not the vanity, it had been plainly partial; first to correct him for grave Cicero, and not for scurril Plautus, whom he confesses to have been reading not long before; next to correct him only, and let so many more ancient Fathers wax old in those pleasant and florid studies without the lash of such a tutoring apparition; insomuch that Basil teaches how some good use may be made of Margites, a sportful poem not now extant writ by Homer; and why not then of Morgante, an Italian romance much to the same purpose?

But if it be agreed we shall be tried by visions, there is a vision recorded by Eusebius, far ancienter than this tale of Jerome to the nun Eustochium, and, besides, has nothing of a fever in it. Dionysius Alexandrinus was, about the year 240, a person of great name in the Church for piety and learning, who customarily availed himself much against heretics by being conversant in their books; until a certain presbyter laid it scrupulously to his conscience, how he dared venture himself among those defiling volumes. The worthy man, loath to give offence, fell into a new debate with himself what was to be thought; when suddenly a vision sent from God (it is his own Epistle that so avers it) confirmed him in these words: "Read any books whatever come to your hands, for you are sufficient both to judge aright and to examine each matter." To this revelation he assented the sooner, as he confesses, because it was answerable to that of the Apostle to the Thessalonians: "Prove all things, hold fast that which is good." And he might have added another remarkable saying of the same author: "To the pure, all things are pure"; not only meats and drinks, but all kind of knowledge whether of good or evil; the knowledge cannot defile, nor consequently the books, if the will and conscience be not defiled. For books are as meats and viands are — some of good, some of evil substance — and yet God in that unapocryphal vision said without exception, "Rise, Peter, kill and eat," leaving the choice to each person's discretion. Wholesome meats to a vitiated stomach differ little or nothing from unwholesome, and best books to a naughty mind are not unappliable to occasions of evil. Bad meats will scarce breed good nourishment in the healthiest concoction; but herein the difference is of bad books, that they to a discreet and judicious reader serve in many respects to discover, to confute, to forewarn, and to illustrate. Whereof what better witness can you expect I should produce than one of your own now sitting in Parliament, the chief of learned men reputed in this land, Mr. Selden; whose volume of natural and national laws proves, not only by great authorities brought together, but by exquisite reasons and theorems almost mathematically demonstrative, that all opinions, yea errors, known, read, and collated, are of main service and assistance toward the speedy attainment of what is truest. I conceive, therefore, that when God did enlarge the universal diet of the human body, saving ever the rules of temperance, he then also, as before, left arbitrary the dieting and repasting of our minds; as wherein every mature person might have to exercise his own leading capacity.

How great a virtue is temperance, how much of moment through the whole life of Man! Yet God commits the managing so great a trust, without particular law or prescription, wholly to the demeanor of every grown person. And therefore, when he himself tabled the Jews from heaven, that omer, which was every man's daily portion of manna, is computed to have been more than might have well sufficed the heartiest feeder thrice as many meals. For those actions which enter into a man, rather than issue out of him, and therefore defile not, God uses not to captivate under a perpetual childhood of prescription, but trusts him with the gift of reason to be his own chooser; there were but little work left for preaching, if law and compulsion should grow so fast upon those things which heretofore were governed only by exhortation. Solomon informs us that much reading is a weariness to the flesh; but neither he nor other inspired author tells us that such or such reading is unlawful; yet certainly had God thought good to limit us herein, it had been much more expedient to have told us what was unlawful, than what was wearisome. As for the burning of those Ephesian books by St. Paul's converts; 'tis replied the books were magic, the Syriac so renders them. It was a private act, a voluntary act, and leaves us to a voluntary imitation: the men in remorse burnt those books which were their own; the magistrate by this example is not appointed; these men practised the books, another might perhaps have read them in some sort usefully.

Good and evil we know in the field of this world grow up together almost inseparably; and the knowledge of good is so involved and interwoven with the knowledge of evil, and in so many cunning resemblances hardly to be discerned, that those confused seeds which were imposed upon Psyche as an incessant labor to cull out, and sort asunder, were not more intermixed. It was from out the rind of one apple tasted, that the knowledge of good and evil, as two twins cleaving together, leaped forth into the world. And perhaps this is that doom which Adam fell into of knowing good and evil, that is to say, of knowing good by evil.

As therefore the state of humanity now is, what wisdom can there be to choose, what continence to forbear without the knowledge of evil? He that can apprehend and consider vice with all his baits and seeming pleasures, and yet abstain, and yet distinguish, and yet prefer that which is truly better, he is the true wayfaring Christian. I cannot praise a fugitive and cloistered virtue, unexercised and unbreathed, that never sallies out and sees his adversary, but slinks out of the race where that immortal garland is to be run for, not without dust and heat.

Assuredly we bring not innocence into the world, we bring impurity much rather: that which purifies us is trial, and trial is by what is contrary. That virtue therefore which is but a youngling in the contemplation of evil, and knows not the utmost that vice promises to his followers, and rejects it, is but a blank virtue, not a pure; his whiteness is but an excremental whiteness; which was the reason why one sage and serious poet, Spenser, whom I dare be known to think a better teacher than Scotus or Aquinas, describing true temperance under the person of Guyon, brings him in with his palmer through the cave of Mammon and the bower of earthly bliss, that he might see and know, and yet abstain. Since therefore, the knowledge and survey of vice is in this world so necessary to the constituting of human virtue, and the scanning of error to the confirmation of truth, how can we more safely, and with less danger, scout into the regions of sin and falsity, than by reading all manner of tractates and hearing all manner of reason? And this is the benefit which may be had of books promiscuously read.

But of the harm that may result hence, three kinds are usually reckoned. First is feared the infection that may spread; but then all human learning and controversy in religious points must remove out of the world, even the Bible itself; for that often relates blasphemy not nicely, it describes the carnal sense of wicked people not inelegantly, it brings in holiest persons passionately murmuring against providence through all the arguments of Epicurus; in other great disputes it answers dubiously and darkly to the common reader. And ask a Talmudist what ails the modesty of his marginal Keri [text as spoken], that Moses and all the prophets cannot persuade him to pronounce the textual Chetiv [written text]. For these causes we all know the Bible itself put by the Papist into the first rank of prohibited books. The most ancient Fathers must be next removed, as Clement of Alexandria, and that Eusebian book of Evangelic preparation transmitting our ears through a board of heathenish obscenities to receive the Gospel. Who finds not that Irenaeus, Epiphanius, Jerome, and others discover more heresies than they well confute, and that often for heresy which is the truer opinion?

Nor boots it to say for these and all the heathen writers of greatest infection, if it must be thought so, with whom is bound up the life of human learning, that they writ in an unknown tongue, so long as we are sure those languages are known as well to the worst of persons, who are both most able and most diligent to instil the poison they suck, first into the courts of princes, acquainting them with the cboicest delights, and criticisms of sin. As perhaps did that Petronius whom Nero called his Arbiter, the master of his revels; and that notorious ribald of Arezzo [Pietro Aretino], dreaded and yet dear to the Italian courtiers. I name not him for posterity's sake, whom Harry VIII named in merriment his Vicar of Hell. By which compendious way all the contagion that foreign books can infuse, will find a passage to the people far easier and shorter than an Indian voyage, though it could be sailed either by the north of Cathay eastward, or of Canada westward, while our Spanish licensing gags the English press never so severely.

But, on the other side, that infection which is from books of controversy in religion, is more doubtful and dangerous to the learned than to the ignorant; and yet those books must be permitted untouched by the licenser. It will be hard to instance where any ignorant man has been ever seduced by papistical book in English, unless it were commended and expounded to him by some of that clergy; and indeed all such tractates, whether false or true, are as the prophecy of Isaiah was to the eunuch, "not to be understood without a guide." But of our priests and doctors how many have been corrupted by studying the comments of Jesuits and Sorbonists, and how fast they could transfuse that corruption into the people, our experience is both late and sad. It is not forgot, since the acute and distinct Arminius was perverted merely by the perusing of a nameless discourse written at Delft, which at first he took in hand to confute.

Seeing, therefore, that those books, and those in great abundance, which are most likely to taint both life and doctrine, cannot be suppressed without the fall of learning, and of all ability in disputation; and that these books of either sort are most and soonest catching to the learned, from whom to the common people whatever is heretical or dissolute may quickly be conveyed; and that evil manners are as perfectly learned without books a thousand other ways which cannot be stopped; and evil doctrine not with books can propagate, except a teacher guide, which he might also do without writing, and so beyond prohibiting: I am not able to unfold how this cautelous enterprise of licensing can be exempted from the number of vain and impossible attempts. And he who were pleasantly disposed, could not well avoid to liken it to the exploit of that gallant man who thought to pound up the crows by shutting his park gate.

Besides another inconvenience, if learned men be the first receivers out of books and dispreaders both of vice and error, how shall the licensers themselves be confided in, unless we can confer upon them, or they assume to themselves above all others in the land, the grace of infallibility and uncorruptedness? And again, if it be true that a wise man, like a good refiner, can gather gold out of the drossiest volume, and that a fool will be a fool with the best book, yes or without book, there is no reason that we should deprive a wise man of any advantage to his wisdom, while we seek to restrain from a fool that which being restrained will be no hindrance to his folly. For if there should be so much exactness always used to keep that from him which is unfit for his reading, we should, in the judgment of Aristotle not only, but of Solomon and of our Saviour, not vouchsafe him good precepts, and by consequence not willingly admit him to good books; as being certain that a wise man will make better use of an idle pamphlet than a fool will do of sacred Scripture.

'Tis next alleged we must not expose ourselves to temptations without necessity, and, next to that, not employ our time in vain things. To both these objections one answer will serve, out of the grounds already laid; that to all men such books are not temptations nor vanities, but useful drugs and materials wherewith to temper and compose effective and strong medicines which Man's life cannot lack. The rest, as children and childish men, who have not the art to qualify and prepare these working minerals, well may be exhorted to forbear, but hindered forcibly they cannot be by all the licensing that sainted Inquisition could ever yet contrive. Which is what I promised to deliver next: that this order of licensing conduces nothing to the end for which it was framed; and has almost prevented me by being clear already, while thus much has been explaining. See the ingenuity of Truth, who, when he gets a free and willing hand, opens himself faster than the pace of method and discourse can overtake him.

It was the task which I began with, to show that no nation, or well instituted state, if they valued books at all, did ever use this way of licensing; and it might be answered, that this is a piece of prudence lately discovered. To which I return, that as it was a thing slight and obvious to think on, so if it had been difficult to find out, there did not lack among them long since who suggested such a course; which they not following, leave us a pattern of their judgment that it was not the not-knowing, but the not-approving, which was the cause of their not using it.

Plato, a man of high authority indeed, but least of all for his commonwealth, in the book of his Laws, which no city ever yet received, fed his fancy with making many edicts to his airy burgomasters, which they who otherwise admire him, wish had been rather buried and excused in the genial cups of an Academic night-sitting. By which laws he seems to tolerate no kind of learning, but by unalterable decree, consisting most of practical traditions, to the attainment whereof a library of smaller bulk than his own Dialogues would be abundant. And there also enacts that no poet should so much as read to any private man what he had written, until the judges and lawkeepers had seen it and allowed it; but that Plato meant this law peculiarly to that commonwealth which he had imagined, and to no other, is evident. Why was he not else a lawgiver himself, but a transgressor, and to be expelled by his own magistrates; both for the wanton epigrams and dialogues which he made, and his perpetual reading of Sophron, Mimus, and Aristophanes, books of grossest infamy; and also for commending the latter of them, though he were the malicious libeller of his chief friends, to be read by the tyrant Dionysius, who had little need of such trash to spend his time on? But that he knew this licensing of poems had reference and dependence to many other provisos there set down in his fancied Republic, which in this world could have no place; and so neither he himself, nor any magistrate, or city ever imitated that course, which, taken apart from those other collateral injunctions, must certainly be vain and fruitless. For if they fell upon one kind of strictness, unless their care were equal to regulate all other things of like aptness to corrupt the mind, that single endeavor they knew would be but a fond labor; to shut and fortify one gate against corruption, and be necessitated to leave others round about wide open.

If we think to regulate printing, thereby to rectify manners, we must regulate all recreations and pastimes, all that is delightful to Man. No music must be heard, no song be set or sung, but what is grave and Doric. There must be licensing dancers, that no gesture, motion, or deportment be taught our youth, but what by their allowance shall be thought honest; for such Plato was provided of. It will ask more than the work of twenty licensers to examine all the lutes, the violins, and the guitars in every house; they must not be suffered to prattle as they do, but must be licensed what they may say. And who shall silence all the airs and madrigals that whisper softness in chambers? The windows also, and the balconies must be thought on; there are shrewd books, with dangerous frontispieces, set to sale; who shall prohibit them? Shall twenty licensers? The villages also must have their visitors to inquire what lectures the bagpipe and the rebeck reads even to the balladry, and the gamut of every municipal fiddler, for these are the countryman's Arcadias, and his Monte Mayors.

Next, what more national corruption, for which England hears ill abroad, than household gluttony? Who shall be the rectors of our daily rioting? And what shall be done to inhibit the multitudes that frequent those houses where drunkenness is sold and harbored? Our garments also should be referred to the licensing of some more sober workmasters, to see them cut into a less wanton garb. Who shall regulate all the mixed conversation of our youth, male and female together, as is the fashion of this country? Who shall still appoint what shall be discoursed, what presumed, and no further? Lastly, who shall forbid and separate all idle resort, all evil company? These things will be, and must be; but how they shall be least hurtful, how least enticing, herein consists the grave and governing wisdom of a state.

To sequester out of the world into Atlantic and Utopian polities, which never can be drawn into use, will not mend our condition; but to ordain wisely as in this world of evil, in the midst whereof God has placed us unavoidably. Nor is it Plato's licensing of books will do this, which necessarily pulls along with it so many other kinds of licensing as will make us all both ridiculous and weary, and yet frustrate; but those unwritten, or at least unconstraining, laws of virtuous education, religious and civil nurture, which Plato there mentions as the bonds and ligaments of the commonwealth, the pillars and the sustainers of every written statute; these they be which will bear chief sway in such matters as these, when all licensing will be easily eluded. Impunity and remissness, for certain, are the bane of a commonwealth; but here the great art lies, to discern in what the law is to bid restraint and punishment, and in what things persuasion only is to work.

If every action which is good or evil in Man at ripe years, were to be under pittance and prescription and compulsion, what were virtue but a name, what praise could be then due to well-doing, what gramercy to be sober, just, or continent? Many there be that complain of divine Providence for suffering Adam to transgress. Foolish tongues! when God gave him reason, He gave him freedom to choose, for reason is but choosing; he had been else a mere artificial Adam, such an Adam as he is in the motions [puppet shows]. We ourselves esteem not of that obedience, or love, or gift, which is of force. God, therefore, left him free, set before him a provoking object, ever almost in his eyes; herein consisted his merit, herein the right of his reward, the praise of his abstinence. Wherefore did He create passions within us, pleasures round about us, but that these rightly tempered are the very ingredients of virtue?

They are not skilful considerers of human things, who imagine to remove sin by removing the matter of sin. For, besides that it is a huge heap increasing under the very act of diminishing, though some part of it may for a time be withdrawn from some persons, it cannot from all, in such a universal thing as books are; and when this is done, yet the sin remains entire. Though you take from a covetous man all his treasure, he has yet one jewel left — you cannot bereave him of his covetousness. Banish all objects of lust, shut up all youth into the severest discipline that can be

22

exercised in any hermitage, you cannot make them chaste, that came not there so: such great care and wisdom is required to the right managing of this point. Suppose we could expel sin by this means; look how much we thus expel of sin, so much we expel of virtue: for the matter of them both is the same; remove that, and you remove them both alike.

This justifies the high providence of God, who, though He command us temperance, justice, continence, yet pours out before us, even to a profuseness, all desirable things, and gives us minds that can wander beyond all limit and satiety. Why should we then affect a rigor contrary to the manner of God and of nature, by abridging or scanting those means which books freely permitted are, both to the trial of virtue, and the exercise of truth? It would be better done to learn that the law must surely be frivolous which goes to restrain things uncertainly and yet equally working to good and to evil. And were I the chooser, a dram of well-doing should be preferred before many times as much the forcible hindrance of evildoing. For God sure esteems the growth and completing of one virtuous person more than the restraint of ten vicious.

And though whatever thing we hear or see, sitting, walking, travelling, or conversing, may be fitly called our book, and is of the same effect that writings are; yet grant the thing to be prohibited were only books, it appears that this order up to the present is far insufficient to the end which it intends. Do we not see — not once or oftener, but weekly — that continued court libel [Mercurius Aulicus, Court Mercury published by King Charles from Oxford] against the Parliament and City printed, as the wet sheets can witness, and dispersed among us, for all that licensing can do? Yet this is the prime service a man would think, wherein this Order should give proof of itself. If it were executed, you'll say. But certain, if execution be remiss or blindfold now, and in this particular, what will it be hereafter and in other books? If then the Order shall not be vain and frustrate, behold a new labor, Lords and Commons. you must repeal and proscribe all scandalous and unlicensed books already printed and divulged (after you have drawn them up into a list, that all may know which are condemned and which not) and ordain that no foreign books be delivered out of custody till they have been read over. This office will require the whole time of not a few overseers, and those no vulgar persons. There be also books which are partly useful and excellent, partly culpable and pernicious; this work will ask as many more officials to make expurgations and expunctions, that the commonwealth of learning be not damnified. In short, when the multitude of books increase upon their hands, you must be ready to catalogue all those printers who are found frequently offending, and forbid the importation of their whole suspected typography. In a word, that this your Order may be exact and not deficient, you must reform it perfectly according to the model of Trent and Seville, which I know you abhor to do.

Yet, though you should condescend to this, which God forbid, the Order still would be but fruitless and defective to that end whereto you meant it. If to prevent sects and schisms, who is so unread or so uncatechized in story that has not heard of many sects refusing books as a hindrance, and preserving their doctrine unmixed for many ages, only by unwritten traditions? The Christian faith, for that was once a schism, is not unknown to have spread all over Asia, before any Gospel or Epistle was seen in writing. If the amendment of manners be aimed at, look into Italy and Spain, whether those places be one scruple the better, the honester, the wiser, the chaster, since all the inquisitional rigor that has been executed upon books.

Another reason whereby to make it plain that this Order will miss the end it seeks, consider by the quality which ought to be in every licenser. It cannot be denied but that he who is made judge to sit upon the birth or death of books, whether they may be wafted into the world or not, had need to be a man above the common measure, both studious, learned, and judicious. There may be else no mean mistakes in the censure of what is passable or not, which is also no mean injury. If he be of such worth as is required, there cannot be a more tedious and unpleasing journey-work, a greater loss of time levied upon his head, than to be made the perpetual reader of unchosen books and pamphlets, oft times huge volumes. There is no book that is acceptable unless at certain seasons; but to be enjoined the reading of that at all times, and in a hand scarce legible, whereof three pages would not down at any time in the fairest print, is an imposition which I cannot believe how he that values time and his own studies, or is but of a sensible nostril, should be able to endure. In this one thing I crave leave of the present licensers to be pardoned for so thinking; who doubtless took this office up, looking on it through their obedience to the Parliament, whose command perhaps made all things seem easy and unlaborious to them; but that this short trial has wearied them out already, their own expressions and excuses to them who make so many journeys to solicit their license, are testimony enough. Seeing, therefore, those who now possess the employment, by all evident signs wish themselves well rid of it, and that no person of worth, none that is not a plain unthrift of his own hours, is ever likely to succeed them, except hu mean to put himself to the salary of a press corrector, we may easily foresee what kind of licensers we are to expect hereafter, either ignorant, imperious, and remiss, or basely pecuniary. This is what I had to show, wherein this Order cannot conduce to that end whereof it bears the intention.

I lastly proceed from the no good it can do, to the manifest hurt it causes in being, first, the greatest discouragement and affront that can be offered to learning and to learned men.

It was the complaint and lamentation of prelates, upon every least breath of a motion to remove pluralities and distribute more equally church revenues, that then all learning would be forever dashed and discouraged. But as for that opinion, I never found cause to think that the tenth part of learning stood or fell with the clergy; nor could I ever but hold it for a sordid and unworthy speech of any churchman who had a competency left him. If, therefore, you be loath to dishearten utterly and discontent, not the mercenary crew of false pretenders to learning, but the free and ingenuous sort of such as evidently were born to study and love learning for itself, not for lucre, or any other end but the service of God and of truth, and perhaps that lasting fame and perpetuity of praise which God and good men have consented shall be the reward of those whose published labors advance the good of mankind; then know, that so far to distrust the judgment and the honesty of one who has but a common repute in learning, and never yet offended, as not to count him fit to print his mind without a tutor and examiner, lest he should drop a schism, or something of corruption, is the greatest displeasure and indignity to a free and knowing spirit that can be put upon him.

What advantage is it to be a man over it is to be a boy at school, if we have only escaped the ferula [switch] to come under the fescue [club] of an Imprimatur; if serious and elaborate writings, as if they were no more than the theme of a grammar-boy under his pedagogue, must not be uttered without the cursory eyes of a temporizing and extemporizing licenser? He who is not trusted with his own actions, his drift not being known to be evil, and standing to the hazard of law and penalty, has no great argument to think himself reputed in the commonwealth wherein he was born for other than a fool or a foreigner. When a man writes to the world, he summons up all his reason and deliberation to assist him; he searches, meditates, is industrious, and likely consults and confers with his judicious friends, after all which done he takes himself to be informed in what he writes, as well as any that wrote before him. If in this the most consummate act of his fidelity and ripeness, no years, no industry, no former proof of his abilities can bring him to that state of maturity as not to be still mistrusted and suspected unless he carry all his considerate diligence, all his midnight watchings, and expense of Palladian oil, to the hasty view of an unleisured licenser, perhaps much his younger, perhaps far his inferior in judgment, perhaps one who never knew the labor of bookwriting, and if he be not repulsed or slighted, must appear in print like a puny with his guardian and his censor's hand on the back of his title to be his bail and surety that he is no idiot or seducer; it cannot be but a dishonor and derogation to the author, to the book, to the privilege and dignity of learning.

And what if the author shall be one so copious of fancy as to have many things well worth the adding, come into his mind after licensing, while the book is yet under the press, which not seldom happens to the best and most diligent writers; and that perhaps a dozen times in one book. The printer dares not go beyond his licensed copy. So often then must the author trudge to his leave-giver, that those his new insertions may be viewed, and many a jaunt will be made, before that licenser, for it must be the same man, can either be found, or found at leisure. Meanwhile, either the press must stand still, which is no small damage, or the author lose his most accurate thoughts, and send the book forth worse than he had made it, which to a diligent writer is the greatest melancholy and vexation that can befall.

And how can a man teach with authority, which is the life of teaching, how can he be a doctor in his book as he ought to be, or else had better be silent, whenas all he teaches, all he delivers, is but under the tuition, of the correction of his patriarchal licenser to blot or alter what precisely accords not with the hide-bound humor which he calls his judgment? When every acute reader upon the first sight of a pedantic license, will be ready with these like words to ding the book a quoit's distance from him: "I hate a pupil teacher, I endure not an instructor that comes to me under the wardship of an overseeing. fist. I know nothing of the licenser, but that I have his own hand here for his arrogance; who shall warrant me his judgment?" "The State, sir," replies the stationer, but has a quick return: "The State shall be my governors, but not my critics; they may be mistaken in the choice of a licenser, as easily as this licenser may be mistaken in an author; this is some common stuff"; and he might add from Sir Francis Bacon, that "Such authorized books are but the language of the times." For though a licenser should happen to be judicious more than ordinary, which will be a great jeopardy of the next succession, yet his very office, and his commission enjoins him to let pass nothing but what is vulgarly received already.

Nay, which is more lamentable, if the work of any deceased author, though never so famous in his lifetime, and even to this day, come to their hands for license to be printed, or reprinted; if there be found in his book one sentence of a venturous edge, uttered in the height of zeal, and who knows whether it might not be the dictate of a divine spirit, yet not suiting with every low, decrepit humor of their own, though it were Knox himself, the reformer of a kingdom, that spoke it, they will not pardon him their dash; the sense of that great man shall to all posterity be lost, for the fearfulness, or the presumptuous rashness, of a perfunctory licenser. And to what an author this violence has been lately done, and in what book of greatest consequence to be faithfully published, I could now instance, but shall forbear till a more convenient season.

Yet if these things be not resented seriously and timely by them who have the remedy in their power, but that such iron-molds as these shall have authority to gnaw out the choicest periods of most exquisite books, and to commit such a treacherous fraud against the orphan remainders of worthiest men after death, the more sorrow will belong to that hapless race of men whose misfortune it is to have understanding. Henceforth, let no man care to learn, or care to be more than worldly wise; for certainly in higher matters to be ignorant and slothful, to be a common steadfast dunce, will be the only pleasant life, and only in request.

And it is a particular disesteem of every knowing man alive, and most injurious to the written labors and monuments of the dead, so to me it seems an undervaluing and vilifying of the whole nation. I cannot set so light by all the invention, the art, the wit, the grave and solid judgment which is in England, as that it can be comprehended in any twenty capacities how good soever; much less that it should not pass except their superintendence be over it, except it be sifted and strained with their strainers; that it should be uncurrent without their manual stamp. Truth and understanding are not such wares as to be monopolized and traded in by tickets and statutes and standards. We must not think to make a staple commodity of all the knowledge in the land, to mark and license it like our broadcloth and our woolpacks. What is it but a servitude like that imposed by the Philistines, not to be allowed the sharpening of our own axes and coulters, but we must repair from all quarters to twenty licensing forges? Had anyone written and divulged erroneous things and scandalous to honest life, misusing and forfeiting the esteem had of his reason among people; if, after conviction, this only censure were adjudged him, that he should never henceforth write, but what were first examined by an appointed officer, whose hand should be annexed to pass his credit for him, that now he might be safely read; it could not be apprehended less than a disgraceful punishment. Therefore, to include the whole nation, and those that never yet thus offended, under such a diffident and suspectful prohibition, may plainly be understood what a disparagement it is. So much the more, when debtors and delinquents may walk abroad without a keeper, but unoffensive books must not stir forth without a visible jailor in their title.

Nor is it to the common people less than a reproach; for if we be so jealous over them as that we dare not trust them with an English pamphlet, what do we but censure them for a giddy, vicious, and ungrounded people; in such a sick and weak state of faith and discretion, as to be able to take nothing down but through the pipe of a licenser? That this is care or love of them, we cannot pretend, when in those popish places where the laity are most hated and despised, the same strictness is used over them. Wisdom we cannot call it, because it stops but one breach of license, nor that neither; when those corruptions which it seeks to prevent, break in faster at other doors which cannot be shut.

And in conclusion, it reflects to the disrepute of our ministers also, of whose labors we should hope better, and of the proficiency which their flock reaps by them, than that after all this light of the Gospel which is and is to be, and all this continual preaching, they should be still frequented with such an unprincipled, unedified, and laic rabble, as that the whiff of every new pamphlet should stagger them out of their catechism and Christian walking. This may have much reason to discourage the ministers, when such a low conceit is had of all their exhortations and the benefiting of their hearers, as that they are not thought fit to be turned loose to three sheets of paper without a licenser; that all the sermons, all the lectures preached, printed, vented in such numbers, and such volumes, as have now well-nigh made all other books unsaleable, should not be armor enough against one single enchiridion, without the castle St. Angelo of an Imprimatur.

And lest some should persuade you, Lords and Commons, that these arguments of learned men's discouragement at this your Order are mere flourishes, and not real, I could recount what I have seen and heard in other countries where this kind of inquisition tyrannizes; when I have sat among their learned ones, for that honor I had, and been counted happy to be born in such a place of philosophic freedom as they supposed England was, while themselves did nothing but bemoan the servile condition into which learning among them was brought; that this was it which had damped the glory of Italian wits; that nothing had been there written now these many years but flattery and fustian. There it was that I found and visited the famous Galileo, grown old, a prisoner to the Inquisition for thinking in astronomy otherwise than the Franciscan and Dominican licensers thought. And though I knew that England then was groaning loudest under the prelatical yoke, nevertheless I took it as a pledge of future happiness that other nations were so persuaded of its liberty. Yet was it beyond my hope that those worthies were then breathing in its air, who should be its leaders to such a deliverance as shall never be forgotten by any revolution of time that this world has to finish. When that was once begun, it was as little in my fear, that what words of complaint I heard among learned persons of other parts uttered against the Inquisition, the same I should hear by as learned persons at home uttered in time of Parliament against an Order of licensing; and that so generally, that when I had disclosed myself a companion of their discontent, I might say, if without envy, that he [Cicero] whom an honest quaestorsbip had endeared to the Sicilians, was not more by them importuned against Verres, than the favorable opinion which I had among many who honor you, and are known and respected by you, loaded me with entreaties and persuasions that I would not despair to lay together that which just reason should bring into my mind toward the removal of an undeserved slavery upon learning. That this is not, therefore, the disburdening of a particular fancy, but the common grievance of all those who had prepared their minds and studies above the vulgar pitch to advance truth in others, and from others to entertain it, thus much may satisfy.

And in their name I shall for neither friend nor foe conceal what the general murmur is; that if it come to inquisitioning again and licensing, and that we are so timorous of ourselves and so suspicious of everybody as to fear each book and the shaking of every leaf, before we know what the contents are; if some who but of late were little better than silenced from preaching, shall come now to silence us from reading, except what they please, it cannot be guessed what is intended by some but a second tyranny over learning; and will soon put it out of controversy that bishops and presbyters are the same to us both name and thing.

That those evils of prelaty which before from five or six and twenty sees were distributively charged upon the whole people, will now light wholly upon learning, is not obscure to us; since now the pastor of a small unlearned parish, on the sudden shall be exalted archbishop over a large diocese of books, and yet not remove, but keep his other cure too, a mystical pluralist. He who but of late cried down the sole ordination of every novice bachelor of art, and denied sole jurisdiction over the simplest parishioner, shall now at home in his prÃvate chair assume both these over worthiest and most excellent books and ablest authors that write them. This is not, you covenants and protestations that we have made, this is not to put down prelaty; this is but to chop an episcopacy; this is but to translate the palace metropolitan from one kind of dominion into another; this is but an old canonical sleight of commuting our penance. To startle thus quickly at a mere unlicensed pamphlet will after a while be afraid of every conventicle, and a while after will make a conventicle of every Christian meeting. But I am certain that a state governed by the rules of justice and fortitude, or a church built and founded upon the rock of faith and true knowledge, cannot be so pusillanimous. While things are yet not constituted in religion, that freedom of writing should be restrained by a discipline imitated from the prelates, and learned by them from the Inquisition, to shut us up all again into the breast of a licenser, must give cause of doubt and discouragement to all learned and religious persons.

Who cannot but discern the fineness of this politic drift, and who are the contrivers: that while bishops were to be baited down, then all presses might be open; it was the people's birthright and privilege in time of Parliament, it was the breaking forth of light. But now, the bishops abrogated and voided out of the Church, as if our Reformation sought no more, but to make room for others into their seats under another name, the episcopal arts begin to bud again; the cruise of truth must run no more oil; liberty of printing must be enslaved again under a prelatical cornmission of twenty, the privilege of the people nullified; and, which is worse, the freedom of learning must groan again, and to its old fetters: all this the Parliament yet sitting. Although their own late arguments and defenses against the prelates might remember them that this obstructing violence meets for the most part with an event utterly opposite to the end which it drives at; instead of suppressing sects and schisms, it raises them and invests them with a reputation: "The punishing of wits enhances their authority," says the Viscount St. Albans, "and a forbidden writing is thought to be a certain spark of truth that flies up in the faces of them who seek to tread it out." This Order, therefore, may prove a nursing mother to sects, but I shall easily show how it will be a step-dame to Truth; and first by disenabling us to the maintenance of what is known already.

Well knows he who uses to consider, that our faith and knowledge thrives by exercise, as well as our limbs and complexion. Truth is compared in Scripture to a streaming fountain; if its waters flow not in a perpetual progression, they sicken into a muddy pool of conformity and tradition. A man may be a heretic in the truth; and if he believe things only because his pastor says so, or the Assembly so determines, without knowing other reason, though his belief be true, yet the very truth he holds becomes his heresy.

There is not any burden that some would gladlier post off to another than the charge and care of their religion. There be, who knows not that there be, of Protestants and professors who live and died in as arrant an implicit faith, as any lay papist of Loretto. A wealthy man addicted to his pleasure and to his profits, finds religion to be a traffic so entangled, and of so many piddling accounts, that of all mysteries he cannot skill to keep a stock going upon that trade. What should he do? He would prefer to have the name to be religious, he would rather bear up with his neighbors in that. What does he, therefore, but resolves to give over toiling, and to find himself out some factor to whose care and credit he may commit the whole managing of his religious affairs; some divine of note and estimation that must be. To him he adheres, resigns the whole warehouse of his religion, with all the locks and keys into his custody; and indeed makes the very person of that man his religion; esteems his associating with him a sufficient evidence and commendatory of his own piety. So that a man may say his religion is now no more within himself, but is become a dividual movable, and goes and comes near him, according as that good man frequents the house. He entertains him, gives him gifts, feasts him, lodges him. His religion comes home at night, prays, is liberally supped, and sumptuously laid to sleep, rises, is saluted, and after the malmsey [wine], or some well-spiced brewage, and better breakfasted than he whose morning appetite would have gladly fed on green figs between

Bethany and Jerusalem, his religion walks abroad at eight, and leaves his kind entertainer in the shop trading all day without his religion.

Another sort there be, who, when they hear that all things shall be ordered, all things regulated and settled, nothing written but what passes through the custom-house of certain publicans that have the tonnaging and the poundaging of all free-spoken truth, will straight give themselves up into your hands, make 'em and cut 'em out what religion you please. There be delights, there be recreations and jolly pastimes that will fetch the day about from sun to sun, and rock the tedious year as in a delightful dream. What need they torture their heads with that which others have taken so strictly, and so unalterably into their own purveying? These are the fruits which a dull ease and cessation of our knowledge will bring forth among the people. How goodly, and how to be wished, were such an obedient unanimity as this, what a fine conformity would it starch us all into! Doubtless a staunch and solid piece of framework, as any January could freeze together.

Nor much better will be the consequence even among the clergy themselves. It is no new thing never heard of before, for a parochial minister, who has his reward, and is at his Hercules' pillars in a warm benefice, to be easily inclinable, if he have nothing else that may rouse up his studies, to finish his circuit in an English concordance and a topic folio, the gatherings and savings of a sober graduateship, a harmony and a catena, treading the constant round of certain common doctrinal heads, attended with their uses, motives, marks, and means; out of which, as out of an alphabet or sol-fa, by forming and transforming, joining and disjoining variously a little bookcraft, and two hours' meditation, might furnish him unspeakably to the performance of more than a weekly charge of sermoning; not to reckon up the infinite helps of interlinearies, breviaries, synopses, and other loitering gear.

But as for the multitude of sermons ready printed and piled up on every text that is not difficult, our London trading St. Thomas in his vestry, and add to boot St. Martin and St. Hugh, have not within their hallowed limits more vendible ware of all sorts ready made; so that penury he never need fear of pulpit provision, having where so plenteously to refresh his magazine. But if his rear and flanks be not impaled, if his back door be not secured by the rigid licenser, but that a bold book may now and then issue forth and give the assault to some of his old collections in their trenches; it will concern him then to keep waking, to stand

32

in watch, to set good guards and sentinels about his received opinions, to walk the round and counter-round with his fellow inspectors, fearing lest any of his flock be seduced, who also then would be better instructed, better exercised and disciplined. And God send that the fear of this diligence, which must then be used, do not make us affect the laziness of a licensing church.

For if we be sure we are in the right, and do not hold the truth guiltily — which becomes us not — if we ourselves don't condemn our own weak and frivolous teaching, and the people for an untaught and irreligious, gadding rout, what can be more fair than when a man judicious, learned, and of a conscience, for all that we know, as good as theirs that taught us what we know, shall not privily from house to house, which is more dangerous, but openly by writing, publish to the world what his opinion is, what his reasons, and wherefore that which is now thought cannot be sound? Christ urged it as the way to justify himself that he preached in public; yet writing is more public than preaching; and more easy to refutation, if need be, there being so many whose business and profession merely it is, to be the champions of truth; which if they neglect, what can be imputed but their sloth or inability?

Thus much we are hindered and disinured by this course of licensing toward the true knowledge of what we seem to know. For how much it hurts and hinders the licensers themselves in the calling of their ministry, more than any secular employment, if they will discharge that office as they ought, so that of necessity they must neglect either the one duty or the other, I insist not, because it is a particular, but leave it to their own conscience, how they will decide it there.

There is yet behind of what I purposed to lay open, the incredible loss and detriment that this plot of licensing puts us to. More than if some enemy at sea should stop up all our havens and ports and creeks, it hinders and retards the importation of our richest merchandise, truth. No, it was first established and put in practice by anti-Christian malice and mystery, on set purpose to extinguish, if it were possible, the light of Reformation, and to settle falsehood; little differing from that policy in which the Turk upholds his Al-Koran by the prohibition of printing. 'Tis not denied, but gladly confessed, we are to send our thanks and vows to Heaven, louder than most of nations, for that great measure of truth which we enjoy, especially in those main points between us and the Pope, with his appurtenances the prelates; but he who thinks we are to pitch our tent here, and have attained the utmost prospect of Reformation that the mortal glass wherein we contemplate can show us, till we come to beatific vision, that man by this very opinion declares that he is yet far short of truth.

Truth indeed came once into the world with her divine Master, and was a perfect shape most glorious to look on. But when she ascended, and her apostles after her were laid asleep, then straight arose a wicked race of deceivers, who, as that story goes of the Egyptian Typhon with his conspirators, how they dealt with the good Osiris, took the virgin Truth, hewed her lovely form into a thousand pieces, and scattered them to the four winds. From that time ever since, the sad friends of Truth, such as dared appear, imitating the careful search that Isis made for the mangled body of Osiris, went up and down gathering limb by limb still as they could find them. We have not yet found them all, Lords and Commons, nor ever shall do, till her Master's second coming. He shall bring together every joint and member, and shall mold them into an immortal feature of loveliness and perfection. Suffer not these licensing prohibitions to stand at every place of opportunity, forbidding and disturbing them that continue seeking, that continue to do our obsequies to the torn body of our martyred saint.

We boast our light; but if we look not wisely on the sun itself, it smites us into darkness. Who can discern those planets that are often combust, and those stars of brightest magnitude that rise and set with the sun, until the opposite motion of their orbs bring them to such a place in the firmament, where they may be seen evening or morning? The light which we have gained, was given us, not to be ever staring on, but by it to discover onward things more remote from our knowledge. It is not the unfrocking of a priest, the unmitering of a bishop, and the removing him from the Presbyterian shoulders that will make us a happy nation; no, if other things as great in the Church, and in the rule of life both economical and political, be not looked into and reformed, we have looked so long upon the blaze that Zwinglius and Calvin have beaconed up to us, that we are stark blind. There are those who perpetually complain of schisms and sects, and make it such a calamity that any person dissents from their maxims. 'Tis their own pride and ignorance which causes the disturbing, who neither will hear with meekness, nor can convince, yet all must be suppressed which is not found in their syntagma. They are the troublers, they are the dividers of unity, who neglect and don't permit others to unite those dissevered pieces which are yet wanting to the body of Truth. To be still searching what we don't know by what we know, still closing up truth to truth as we find it (for all her body is homogeneal and proportional), this is the golden rule in theology as well as in arithmetic, and makes up the best harmony in a church; not the forced and outward union of cold and neutral and inwardly divided minds.

Lords and Commons of England, consider what nation it is where you are, and of which you are the governors; a nation not slow and dull, but of a quick, ingenious, and piercing spirit, acute to invent, subtle and sinewy to discourse, not beneath the reach of any point the highest that human capacity can soar to. Therefore the studies of learning in his deepest sciences have been so ancient and so eminent among us, that writers of good antiquity and ablest judgment have been persuaded that even the school of Pythagoras and the Persian wisdom, took beginning from the old philosophy of this island. And that wise and civil Roman, Julius Agricola, who governed once here for Caesar, preferred the natural wits of Britain before the labored studies of the French. Nor is it for nothing that the grave and frugal Transylvanian sends out yearly from as far as the mountainous borders of Russia and beyond the Hercynian wilderness, not their youth but their staid men, to learn our language and our theologic arts.

Yet that which is above all this, the favor and the love of Heaven, we have great argument to think in a peculiar manner propitious and propending towards us. Why else was this nation chosen before any other, that out of it as out of Zion should be proclaimed and sounded forth the first tidings and trumpet of Reformation to all Europe? And had it not been the obstinate perverseness of our prelates against the divine and admirable spirit of Wyclif, to suppress him as a schismatic and innovator, perhaps neither the Bohemian Huss and Jerome (of Prague), no, nor the name of Luther, or of Calvin, had been ever known; the glory of reforming all our neighbors had been completely ours. But now, as our obdurate clergy have with violence demeaned the matter, we are become hitherto the latest and the most backward scholars, of whom God offered to have made us the teachers. Now once again by all concurrence of signs, and by the general instinct of holy and devout people, as they daily and solemnly express their thoughts, God is decreeing to begin some new and great period in His Church, even to the reforming of Reformation itself. What does He then but reveal himself to His servants, and, as His manner is, first to His English? I say as His manner is, first to us, though we mark not the method of His counsels, and are unworthy. Behold now this vast city, a city of refuge, the mansion house of liberty, encompassed and surrounded with His protection. The shop of war has not there more anvils and hammers waking, to fashion out the plates and instruments of armed justice in defense of beleaguered truth, than there are pens and heads there, sitting by their studious lamps, musing, searching, revolving new notions and ideas wherewith to present, as with their homage and their fealty, the approaching Reformation; others as fast reading, trying all things, assenting to the force of reason and convincement. What could a man require more from a nation so pliant and so prone to seek after knowledge? What lacks there to such a towardly and pregnant soil, but wise and faithful laborers, to make a knowing people, a nation of prophets, of sages, and of worthies? We reckon more than five months yet to harvest; there need not be five weeks, had we but eyes to lift up; the fields are white already.

Where there is much desire to learn, there of necessity will be much arguing, much writing, many opinions; for opinion in good men is but knowledge in the making. Under these fantastic terrors of sect and schism, we wrong the earnest and zealous thirst after knowledge and understanding which God has stirred up in this city. What some lament of, we rather should rejoice at, should rather praise this pious forwardness among people, to reassume the ill-deputed care of their religion into their own hands again. A little generous prudence, a little forbearance of one another, and some grain of charity might win all these diligences to join and unite into one general and friendly search after truth; could we but forego this prelatical tradition of crowding free consciences and Christian liberties into canons and precepts of men. I doubt not, if some great and worthy stranger should come among us, wise to discern the mold and temper of a people, and how to govern it, observing the high hopes and aims, the diligent alacrity of our extended thoughts and reasonings in the pursuance of truth and freedom, but that he would cry out as Pyrrhus did, admiring the Roman docility and courage, "If such were my Epirots, I would not despair the greatest design that could be attempted to make a church or kingdom happy."

Yet these are the men cried out against for schismatics and sectaries; as if, while the Temple of the Lord was building, some cutting, some squaring the marble, others hewing the cedars, there should be a sort of irrational person who could not consider there must be many schisms and many dissections made in the quarry and in the timber, before the house of God can be built. And when every stone is laid artfully together, it cannot be united into a continuity, it can but be contiguous in this world; neither can every piece of the building be of one form; but rather the perfection consists in this, that out of many moderate varieties and friendly dissimilitudes that are not vastly disproportional, arises the goodly and the graceful syrnmetry that commends the whole pile and structure.

Let us, therefore, be more considerate builders, more wise in spiritual architecture, when great reformation is expected. For now the time seems come, when Moses, the great prophet, may sit in heaven rejoicing to see that memorable and glorious wish of his fulfilled, when not only our seventy elders, but all the Lordâ€™s people, are become prophets. No marvel then though some men, and some good men too, perhaps, but young in goodness, as Joshua then was, envy them. They fret, and out of their own weakness are in agony, for fear that these divisions and subdivisions will undo us. The adversary again applauds, and waits the hour when they have branched themselves out, says he, small enough into parties and partitions, then will be our time. Fool! he sees not the firm root out of which we all grow, though into branches; nor will beware until he see our small divided maniples cutting through at every angle of his ill-united and unwieldy brigade. And that we are to hope better of all these supposed sects and schisms, and that we shall not need that solicitude, honest perhaps, though over-timorous, of them that vex in this behalf, but shall laugh in the end at those malicious applauders of our differences, I have these reasons to persuade me.

First, when a city shall be as it were besieged and blocked about, its navigable river infested, inroads and incursions round, defiance and battle oft rumored to be marching up even to its walls and suburb trenches; that then the people, or the greater part, more than at other times, wholly taken up with the study of highest and most important matters to be reformed, should be disputing, reasoning, reading, inventing, discoursing, even to a rarity and admiration, things not before discoursed or written of, argues first a singular good will, contentedness and confidence in your prudent foresight, and safe government, Lords and Commons; and from thence derives itself to a gallant bravery and well grounded contempt of their enemies, as if there were no small number of as great spirits among us, as his was, who, when Rome was nigh besieged by Hannibal, being in the city, bought that piece of ground at no cheap rate on which Hannibal himself encamped his own regiment.

Next, it is a lively and cheerful presage of our happy success and victory. For as in a body, when the blood is fresh, the spirits pure and vigorous not only to vital but to rational faculties, and those in the most acute and the most pert operations of wit and subtlety, it argues in what good plight and constitution the body is; so when the cheerfulness of the people is so sprightly up, as that it has, not only that with which to guard well its own freedom and safety, but to spare, and to bestow upon the most solid and most sublime points of controversy and new invention, it betokens us not degenerated nor drooping to a fatal decay, but casting off the old and wrinkled skin of corruption to outlive these pangs, and wax young again, entering the glorious ways of truth and prosperous virtue, destined to become great and honorable in these latter ages.

I think I see in my mind a noble and puissant nation rousing himself like a strong man after sleep, and shaking his invincible locks. I think I see him as an eagle mewing his mighty youth, and kindling his undazzled eyes at the full midday beam; purging and unscaling his long abused sight at the fountain itself of heavenly radiance; while the whole noise of timorous and flocking birds, with those also that love the twilight, flutter about, amazed at what he means, and in their envious gabble would prognosticate a year of sects and schisms.

What would you do then, should you suppress all this flowery crop of knowledge and new light sprung up and yet springing daily in this city? Should you set an oligarchy of twenty engrossers over it, to bring a famine upon our minds again, when we shall know nothing but what is measured to us by their bushel? Believe it, Lords and Commons, they who counsel you to such a suppressing, do as good as bid you suppress yourselves; and I will soon show how. If it be desired to know the immediate cause of all this free writing and free speaking, there cannot be assigned a truer than your own mild and free and humane government. It is the liberty, Lords and Commons, which your own valorous and happy counsels have purchased us, liberty which is the nurse of all great wits. This is that which has rarefied and enlightened our spirits like the influence of heaven; this is that which has enfranchised, enlarged, and lifted up our apprehensions degrees above themselves.

You cannot make us now less capable, less knowing, less eagerly pursuing of the truth, unless you first make yourselves, that made us so, less the lovers, less the founders of our true liberty. We can grow ignorant again, brutish, formal, and slavish, as you found us; but you then must first become that which you cannot be, oppressive, arbitrary, and tyrannous, as they were from whom you have freed us. That our hearts are now more capacious, our thoughts more erected to the search and expectation of greatest and most exact things, is the issue of your own virtue propagated in us. You cannot suppress that unless you reinforce an abrogated and merciless law, that parents may despatch at will their own children. And who shall then stick closest to you, and excite others? Not he who takes up arms for coat and conduct, and his four nobles of Danegelt [taxes]. Although I dispraise not the defense of just immunities, yet love my peace better, if that were all. Give me the liberty to know, to utter, and to argue freely according to conscience, above all liberties

What would be best advised, then, if it be found so hurtful and so unequal to suppress opinions for the newness, or the unsuitableness to a customary acceptance, will not be my task to say. I only shall repeat what I have learned from one of your own honorable number, a right noble and pious Lord, who, had he not sacrificed his life and fortunes to the Church and Commonwealth, we had not now missed and bewailed a worthy and undoubted patron of this argument. You know him I am sure; yet I for honor's sake, and may it be eternal to him, shall name him, the Lord Brooke. He, writing of Episcopacy, and by the way treating of sects and schisms, left you his vote, or rather now the last words of his dying charge (which I know will ever be of dear and honored regard with you) so full of meekness and breathing charity that next to his last testament, who bequeathed love and peace to his disciples, I cannot call to mind where I have read or heard words more mild and peaceful. He there exhorts us to hear with patience and humility those, however they be miscalled, that desire to live purely, in such a use of God's ordinances as the best guidance of their conscience gives them, and to tolerate them, though in some disconformity to ourselves. The book itself will tell us more at large, being published to the world and dedicated to the Parliament by him who, both for his life and for his death, deserves that what advice he left be not laid by without perusal.

And now the time in special is, by privilege to write and speak what may help to the further discussing of matters in agitation. The temple of Janus with his two controversal faces might now not unsignificantly be set open, as if for war. And though all the winds of doctrine were let loose to play upon the earth, so Truth be in the field, we do injuriously by licensing and prohibiting to misdoubt her strength. Let her and Falsehood grapple; who ever knew Truth put to the worse, in a free and open encounter? Her confuting is the best and surest suppressing. He who hears what praying there is for light and clearer knowledge to be sent down among us, would think of other matters to be constituted beyond the discipline of Geneva, framed and fabricked already to our hands. Yet when the new light which we beg for shines in upon us, there are who envy and oppose, if it come not first in at their casements. What a collusion is this, when we are exhorted by the wise man to use diligence, to seek for wisdom as for hidden treasures early and late, that another order shall enjoin us to know nothing but by statute. When a man has been laboring the hardest labor in the deep mines of knowledge, has furnished out his findings in all their equipage, drawn forth his reasons as it were a battle ranged, scattered and defeated all objections in his way, calls out his adversary into the plain, offers him the advantage of wind and sun, if he please; only that he may try the matter by dint of argument, for his opponents then to skulk, to lay ambushments, to keep a narrow bridge of licensing where the challenger should pass, though it be valor enough in soldiership, is but weakness and cowardice in the wars of Truth.

For who knows not that Truth is strong, next to the Almighty? She needs no policies, nor strategems, nor licensings to make her victorious; those are the shifts and the defenses that error uses against her power. Give her but room, and do not bind her when she sleeps, for then she speaks not true, as the old Proteus did, who spake oracles only when he was caught and bound, but rather she turns herself into all shapes except her own, and perhaps tunes her voice according to the time, as Micaiah did before Ahab, until she be adjured into her own likeness. Yet it is not impossible that she may have more shapes than one. What else is all that rank of things indifferent, wherein Truth may be on this side, or on the other, without being unlike herself? What but a vain shadow else is the abolition of those ordinances, that hand-writing nailed to the cross; what great purchase is this Christian liberty which Paul so often boasts of? His doctrine is, that he who eats, or eat from another, though it be not in fundamentals; and through our forwardness to suppress, and our backwardness to recover any enthralled piece of truth out of the grip of custom, we care not to keep truth separated from truth, which is the fiercest rent and disunion of all. We do not see that while we still affect by all means a rigid external formality, we may as soon fall again into a gross conforming stupidity, a stark and dead congealment of "wood, and hay, and stubble" forced and frozen together, which is more to the sudden degenerating of a church than many subdichotomies of petty schisms.

Not that I can think well of every light separation, or that all in a church is to be expected gold and silver and precious stones. It is not possible for Man to sever the wheat from the tares, the good fish from the other fry; that must be the angels' ministry at the end of mortal things. Yet if all cannot be of one mind — as who looks they should be? — this doubtless is more wholesome, more prudent, and more Christian, that many be tolerated, rather than all compelled. I do not mean tolerated popery and open superstition, which, as it extirpates all religions and civil supremacies, so itself should be extirpate, provided first that all charitable and compassionate means be used to win and regain the weak and the misled; that also which is impious or evil absolutely, either against faith or manners, no law can possibly permit, that does not intend to unlaw itself; but those neighboring differences, or rather indifferences, are what I speak of, whether in some point of doctrine or of discipline, which though they may be many, yet need not interrupt the unity of spirit, if we could but find among us the bond of peace.

In the meanwhile, if anyone would write and bring his helpful hand to the slow-moving Reformation which we labor under, if truth have spoken to him before others, or but seemed at least to speak, who has so bejesuited us that we should trouble that man with asking license to do so worthy a deed, and not consider this, that if it come to prohibiting, there is not anything more likely to be prohibited than truth itself; whose first appearance to our eyes bleared and dimmed with prejudice and custom, is more unsightly and unplausible than many errors, even as the person is of many a great one slight and contemptible to see to? And what do they tell us vainly of new opinions, when this very opinion of theirs, that none must be heard but whom they like, is the worst and newest opinion of all others; and is the chief cause why sects and schisms do so much abound, and true knowledge is kept at a distance from us; besides yet a greater danger which is in it?

For when God shakes a kingdom with strong and healthful commotions to a general reforming, it is not untrue that many sectaries and false teachers are then busiest in seducing; but yet more true it is that God then raises to His own work men of rare abilities, and more than common industry, not only to look back and revise what has been taught heretofore, but to gain further and go on, some new enlightened steps in the discovery of truth. For such is the order of God's enlightening His church, to dispense and deal out by degrees His beam, so as our earthly eyes may best sustain it.

Neither is God appointed and confined, where and out of what place these His chosen shall be first heard to speak: for He sees not as a man sees, chooses not as a man chooses, lest we should devote ourselves again to set places, and assemblies, and outward callings of humans; planting our faith one while in the old Convocation house, and another while in the Chapel at Westminster; when all the faith and religion that shall be there canonized, is not sufficient without plain convincement and the charity of patient instruction, to supple the least bruise of conscience, to edify the meanest Christian who desires to walk in the Spirit, and not in the letter of human trust, for all the number of voices that can be there made; no, though Harry VII himself there, with all his liege tombs about him, should lend them voices from the dead, to swell their number.

And if the men be erroneous who appear to be the leading schismatics, what withholds us but our sloth, our self-will, and distrust in the right cause, that we do not give them gentle meetings and gentle dismissions, that we debate not and examine the matter thoroughly with liberal and frequent audience; if not for their sakes, yet for our own? seeing no man who has tasted learning, but will confess the many ways of profiting by those who, not contented with stale receipts, are able to manage and set forth new positions to the world. And were they but as the dust and cinders of our feet, so long as in that notion they may yet serve to polish and brighten the armory of Truth, even for that respect they were not utterly to be cast away. But if they be of those whom God has fitted for the special use of these times with eminent and ample gifts — and those perhaps neither among the priests, nor among the pharisees — and we in the haste of a precipitant zeal shall make no distinction, but resolve to stop their mouths because we fear they come with new and dangerous opinions (as we commonly forejudge them before we understand them); no less than woe to us while thinking thus to defend the Gospel, we are found the persecutors.

There have been not a few since the beginning of this [Long] Parliament (both of the Presbytery and others) who by their unlicensed books, to the contempt of an Imprimatur, first broke that triple ice clung about our hearts) and taught the people to see day. I hope that none of those were the persuaders to renew upon us this bondage which they themselves have wrought so much good by contemning. But if neither the check that Moses gave to young Joshua, nor the countermand which our Savior gave to young John, who was so ready to prohibit those whom he thought unlicensed, be not enough to admonish our elders how unacceptable to God their testy mood of prohibiting is; if neither their own remembrance what evil has abounded in the church by this obstruction of licensing) and what good they themselves have begun by transgressing it, be not enough, but that they will persuade and execute the most Dominican part of the Inquisition over us, and are already with one foot in the stirrup so active at suppressing, it would be no unequal distribution, in the first place, to suppress the suppressors themselves; whom the change of their condition has puffed up, more than their late experience of harder times has made wise.

And as for regulating the press, let no man think to have the honor of advising you better than yourselves have done in that order published next before this, "that no book be printed, unless the printer's and the author's name (or at least the printer's) be registered." Those which otherwise come forth (if they be found mischievous and libellous) the fire and the executioner will be the timeliest and the most effectual remedy that man's prevention can use. For this authentic Spanish policy of licensing books, if I have said anything, will prove the most unlicensed book itself within a short while; and was the immediate image of a Star Chamber decree to that purpose made in those very times when that Court did the rest of those its pious works, for which it is now fallen from the stars with Lucifer. Whereby you may guess what kind of state prudence, what love of the people, what care of religion or good manners there was at the contriving, although with singular hypocrisy it pretended to bind books to their good behavior. And how it got the upper hand of your precedent order so well constituted before, if we may believe those men whose profession gives them cause to inquire most, it may be doubted there was in it the fraud of some old patentees and monopolizers in the trade of bookselling; who under pretense of the poor in their Company not to be defrauded, and the just retaining of each man his several copy[rights], which God forbid should be gainsaid, brought diverse glossing colors to the House, which were indeed but colors, and serving to no end except it be to exercise a superiority over their neighbors; men who do not, therefore, labor in an honest profession to which learning is indebted, that they should be made other men's vassals. Another end is thought was aimed at by some of them in procuring by petition this Order, that having power in their hands, malignant books might the easier escape abroad, as the event shows.

But of these sophisms and refutations of merchandise I skill not. This I know, that errors in good government and in a bad are equally almost incident; for what magistrate may not be misinformed and much the sooner, if liberty of printing be reduced into the power of a few? But to redress willingly and speedily what has been erred, and in highest authority to esteem a plain advertisement more than others have done a sumptuous bribe, is a virtue, honored Lords and Commons, answerable to your highest actions, and whereof none can participate but greatest and wisest men.

Supplement

to

Areopagitica
Freedom of the Press

Sasha Newborn, ed.

Bandanna Books   2011   Santa Barbara

*This Supplement was prepared for use with
John Milton's Areopagitica, Freedom of the Press
Bandanna Books ISBN 0-942208-04-8*

Contents

Preface for Teachers

This supplement is designed to help supply background information, opinions and interpretations of John Milton, *Areopagitica*, and the issue of freedom of the press. Milton's "other" career—poetry, and in particular Paradise Lost—won't be found in this supplement. In fact, Milton remained a pamphleteer until 1655, when he returned to poetry and his greatest glory as an epic poet.

Sections are organized as questions to which a number of "answers" are given. The answers, from many experts, contradict each other, are confused, indirect, or answer a different question entirely. Your job, should you choose to accept it, is to expedite discussion, and perhaps to referee or to reserve judgment entirely. Milton did not solve all our problems by raising the issue. In fact, the importance of this little pamphlet has only increased with time. In our age, legislators can't keep up with every new twist in telecommunications; Milton's battle for freedom of thought is refought every few years in the corridors of power. The device of copyright, which Milton championed, has blossomed into an industry of derivative rights, which enables many artists and writers to sustain themselves by their work. The music industry and the Internet raise new questions on the role of copyright.

Consult the Glossary in the back of this book for definitions of unfamiliar terms, persons or places. The Bibliography lists works cited in this Supplement, and the Notes are linked to text passages in this Supplement Edition of *Areopagitica: Freedom of the Press*, from Bandanna Books.

Why is the *Areopagitica* important?

No better defense of freedom of the press has been written. Milton surveys the history of censorship and licensing through ancient times to his own day, including a personal experience in Italy with Galileo and his friends.

Exchange of ideas—John Milton's essay is an argument defending the value of the exchange of ideas in a democracy through printing. This Reformation idea was aimed at breaking the control over people's minds that the Roman Catholic Church tried to maintain.

Liberty—Milton: "For me, I have determined to lay up as the best treasure and solace of a good old age, if God vouchsafe it me, the honest liberty of free speech from my youth...Liberty has a sharp and double edge, fit only to be handled by just and virtuous men: to bad and dissolute it becomes a mischief unwieldy in their own hands."

Who was John Milton?

In 1644, John Milton was known as a Latin and English poet whose only work had been tutoring family members; he had recently entered politics by pamphleteering about divorce, religion, and education.

Milton had been a poet for ten years after his schooling, utterly nonpolitical, and supported by his father, who had faith in John's abilities. By the 1640s England was embroiled in factionalism, sparked by the adventurism of Charles I. Milton turned his talents to pamphleteering, first for religious freedom, then for liberalization of divorce laws. At the time of Areopagitica's publication, he was known as "Milton the Divorcer."

Milton's account—

> I was born at London of respectable parents. My father was a man of the highest integrity; my mother, an excellent woman, was particularly known thorughout the neighborhood for her charitable donations. My father destined me from a child for the pursuits of polite learning, which I prosecuted with such eagerness that after I was twelve years old I rarely retired to bed from lucubrations till midnight. This was the first thing which proved pernicious to my eyes, to the natural

weakness of which were added frequent headaches. But as all this could not abate my instinctive ardor for learning, he provided me, in addition to the ordinary instructions of the grammar school, masters to give me daily lessons at home. Being thus instructed in various languages, and having gotten no slight taste of the sweetness of philosophy, he sent me to Cambridge, one of our two national colleges. There, aloof from all profligate conduct, and with the approbation of all good men, I studied seven years, according to the usual course of discipline and of scientific instruction—till I obtained, and with applause, the degree of master.... At my father's country house, to which he had retired to pass the remainder of his days, being perfectly at my ease, I gave myself up entirely to reading the Greek and Latin writers.... After passing five years in this way, I had the curiosity, after the death of my mother, to see foreign countries, and above all, Italy."

Who was in Milton's family?

Father disinherited—John Phillips: "The learned Mr. John Milton ... is said to bee descended from an antient Knightly Family in Buckinghamshire.... His Father was entitled a true Nobility ... having bin disinherited about ye beginning of Queen Elizabeths reign by his Father a Romanist ... for reading the Bible.... Hee came yong to London ... and was so prosperous ...as to bee able to breed up in a liberal manner, and provide a competency for two Sons, and a Daughter: After which ... hee gave over his trade, and went to live in the Country."

1608, Dec. 9. Birth of John Milton in London, third of six children.

Father and mother—Wood: "He was born in Breadstreet within the City of London, between 6 and 7 a clock in the morning of the ninth of Decemb. an. 1608.... His father Joh. Milton, who was a Scrivner living at the Spread Eagle in the said street, was a Native of Halton in Oxfordshire, and his mother was named Sarah was of the antient family of the Bradshaws."

Sister and brother—Toland: "John Milton [was] the Son likewise of John Milton, and Sarah Caston, a Woman exemplary for her Liberality to the Poor.... [He had two siblings who lived to adulthood,] Anna marry'd to Edward Philips; and Chrisopher bred to the Common Law ... a man of no Parts or Ability."

What was his childhood like?

Thomas Young tutor—His father hired a tutor, Thomas Young, a Scots Puritan, for his precocious young son to learn French, Italian and Hebrew as well as Latin and Greek. Young John eagerly threw himself into books. At twelve he was writing poetry.

Edward Phillips: "He had ... a Master possibly at his Father's house...Thomas Young, Pastor of the English Company of Merchants at Hamborough."

Outstripping instructors—Toland: "He made an incredible Progress in the knowlege of Words and Things, his Diligence and Inclination outstripping the care of his Instructors. After the twelfth Year of his Age, such was his insatiable thirst for Learning, he seldom went to bed before midnight. This was the first undoing of his Eys, to whose natural debility were added frequent Headachs, which could not retard or extinguish his laudable Passion for Letters."

1620. Enters St. Paul's school at 12.

In St. Paul's—Wood: "He ... was educated mostly in Pauls school under Alex. Gill senior, and thence at 15 years of age was sent to Christs Coll. in Cambridge, where he was put under the tuition of Will. Chappell, afterwards Bishop of Ross in Ireland."

What happened during Milton's college career?

Enters college—1625. Enters college at 15 years old. Milton wrote Latin and English poems, and declared himself opposed to the medieval disputation system of education then current in Cambridge. "Lady" Milton, as he was called, was unpopular with schoomates at first.

Rise of Laud—Haller: Charles I came to the throne at the moment when Milton was entering Cambridge. Laud had since that time been rising step by step, and he had made his power felt at Cambridge as he had done before at Oxford. Directly after Milton's departure from the university, Laud became archbishop.... Indeed, the main strength of the spiritual brotherhood had already begun to ebb at Cambridge when Milton arrived there."

Suspended from Cambridge—Hanford: "The poet's rustication in consequence of a quarrel with his University tutor ... marks an important moment in the breaking down of the carefully schooled docility of Milton's boyhood. The fact of a real and fundamental change in the poet's experience is confirmed by all that we know of his relations to the University."

Priestly education—But with a flair for florid speeches he won plaudits and school friendships, in particular with Charles Diodati. He gave up his early intention of becoming an Anglican priest, offended at his fellow students' attitudes. At Cambridge his religious beliefs were middle of the road Anglican—Puritan but not Calvinist, and certainly not a fan of Archbishop Laud, a back-pedaller toward Catholicism.

Declines Orders—1629, March 20. Milton takes a B.A. degree. He declines taking religious Orders. Charles I dissolves Parliament for the next eleven years.

Perjure or split faith—Milton: "He who would take Orders must subscribe slave and take an oath withall, which unlesse he took with a conscience that would retch, he must either perjure or split faith. ... [I] thought it better to preserve a blameless silence."

Milton's profession—Haller: "Milton ... arrived at the university supremely confident of himself, possessed by love of learning and the gift for poetry. His intention was to prepare for the pulpit. Literature, in the seventeenth century, was not yet regarded as a profession in itself sufficient for a man of Milton's social position. The English poets of the preceding age had been public men, courtiers and playwrights with now and then a country gentleman or parson. Milton's profession was to be the church, and his formal education was of the sort universally regarded as appropriate to that end. The outcome was that he abandoned the church and its pulpit in favor of literature and the press, but with no flagging of his youthful ambition to be a great teacher of religion and morality."

Chooses literature—1632, July. Milton receives an M.A. degree. His essay "On Shakespear" appears in the Second Folio printing of Shakespeare's plays.

How did Milton prepare himself after college?

Poetry—After graduation, he resolves for no profession except poetry, and prepares himself intensely in study of the classical world, music, astronomy, Italian literature.

Studies Latin and Greek—Wood: "After he had taken the degrees in Arts, he left the University of his own accord, and was not expelled for misdemeanors, as his Adversaries have said. Where upon retiring to his Fathers house in the Country, he spent some time in turning over Latin and Greek Authors, and now and then made excursions into the great City to buy books."

Milton's particular task—Haller: "The result of all this was that Milton at the age of twenty-three went from Cambridge to spend six years at his father's house at Horton. His life there was conducted according to plan. Cambridge, if it taught him anything, taught him that he must take time to learn much more than could be learned there.... The particular task he set himself at Horton was to read the ancient writers and to go through history 'in the method of time.' Beginning with Greece and Rome, he came down through Constantine to the Christian centuries, to the fathers and councils, the Italian cities, and finally the Reformation and England."

Not nice—Richardson: "Whatever he Undertook was Dispatch'd as soon as possible. He was Always in Hast.... Milton was not Nice, but took what was Set before him. All kinds of Strong Liquors he Hated."

No delay—Milton: "For me such is the impetuosity of my temper, that no delay, no quiet, no different care and thought of almost any thing else, can stop me 'till I come to journey's end, and finish the present study to the utmost I am able."

1637. *Lycidas* and *Comus* published.

Skilled with a sword—Wood: "He was of a moderate Stature, and well-proportioned, of a ruddy complexion, light brown hair and handsome features; save that his eyes were none of the quickest ... and his gate [sic] erect and manly, bespeaking courage and undauntedness.... He wore a sword while he had his sight, and was skilled in using it. He had an excellent ear."

What happened on Milton's trip to Italy?

1638, April. Milton, "a figure obscure," travels to Italy.

Visits Paris—Wood: "He touched at Paris ... became known to Hugo Grotius, then and there Embassador from the Qu. of Sweden; but the manners and genius of that place being not agreeable to his mind, he soon left it."

Wits of Florence—John Phillips: "Hasting to Italy ... hee arriv'd at Florence. Here hee liv'd two moneths in familiar & elegant conversation with the choice Witts of that Citty, and was admitted by them to thir private Academies; an Oeconomy much practis'd among the Virtuosi of those parts, for the communication of

Polite literature, as well as for the cementing of friendships."

Italian friends—Edward Phillips: "He was soon taken notice of by the most Learned and Ingenious of the Nobility, and the Grand Wits of Florence, who caress'd him with all the Honours and Civilities imaginable; particularly Jacobo Gaddi, Carolo Dati, Antonio Francini, Frescobaldo, Cultellino, Bonmatthei and Clementillo: Whereof Gaddi hath a large Elegant Italian Canzonet in his Praise: Dati, a Latin Epistle; both Printed before his Latin Poems, together with a Latin Distich of the Marquess of Villa, and another of Selvaggi, and a Latin Tetrastick of Giovanni Salsilli, a Roman."

Visit to Galileo—Toland: "I forgot all this while to mention that he paid a Visit to Galileo, then an old man, and Prisoner to the Inquisition for thinking otherwise in Astronomy than pleas'd the Franciscan Friers."

Rome and Naples—John Phillips: "From Florence hee went to Rome, where, as in all places, hee spent his time in the choicest company; and amongst others there, in that of Lucas Holstein. At Naples, which was his next remove, hee became acquainted wth Marquis Manso, a learned Person, and so aged as to have bin Contemporary and intimate with Torquato Tasso, the famous Italian Heroic.... From Rome hee revisited Florence for the sake of his charming friends there; and then proceeded to Venice.... Thence through France hee returnd home, having, with no ill management of his time, spent about fifteen moneths abroad."

Consulted on Italian—Richardson: "So remarkable was he for his Knowledge in the Italian Tongue that the Crusca (an Academy Set up for the Reducing, and keeping the Florentine Language to its First Purity) made no Scruple to Consult Him, Whom they had receiv'd an Academician, on Difficult and Controverted Points."

Did Milton change on returning to England?

Hurries home—1639, August. Milton hurries home on hearing of political turmoil.

Politics—1640. Milton the poet begins tutoring, but is drawn into politics. April-May: Short Parliament. Autumn: Long Parliament.

Nephews—John Phillips: "Hee had from his first settling taken care of instructing his two Nephews by his Sister Phillips." These nephews are John Phillips and Edward Phillips, both of whom wrote biographies of him later (see Bibliography).

Person of wonderful parts—Wood: "At first we find him a Presbyterian and a most sharp and violent opposer of Prelacy, the established ecclesiastical Discipline and the orthodox Clergy.... Shortly after he did set on foot and maintained very odd and novel Positions concerning Divorce, and then taking part with the Independents, he became a great Antimonarchist, a bitter Enemy to K. Ch. I.... Afterwards being made Latin Secretary to the Parliament, we find him a Commonwealths man.... To conclude, he was a person of wonderful parts, of a very sharp, biting and satyrical wit."

First pamphlet—1641. Milton's first political pamphlet, *On Reformation in England.* Milton resides on Aldersgate Street.

1642. Civil war begins.

Not in army—Masson: At no time from the actual commencement of the war was Milton out with the Parliamentarian army. I am sorry that such was the fact, and cannot quite account for it.... I believe there is some unascertained reason why he did not do so, and that the reason is not merely that he still preferred the Muses to Mars."

Milton:

When the Assault was intended to the City.

Captain, or Colonel, or Knight in arms,
Whose chance on these defenceless doors may seize,
If deed of honour did thee ever please,
Guard them, and him within protect from harms.

He can requite thee; for he knows the charms
That call fame on such gentle acts as these,
And he can spread thy name o'er lands and seas,
Whatever clime the sun's bright circle warms.

Lift not thy speak against the Muses' bower:
The great Emathian conqueror bid spare
The house of Pindarus when temple and tower

Went to the ground; and the repeated air
Of sad Electra's poet had the power
To save the Athenian walls from ruin bare.

Nailed to the door?—Masson: "Did Milton actually nail up, or paste up, such a thing as this outside his door in Aldersgate Street, on the 12th or 13th of November 1642, and himself remain within-doors? ... How was an ordinary Cavalier Captain to know that 'the great Emathian Conqueror' was Alexander the Great, and that 'sad Electra's poet' was Euripides?"

War at a distance—1643. Masson: "The war having rolled away from London, Milton sat on untroubled in his house in Aldersgate Street through the winter of 1642–43 and the spring of 1643. The teaching of his nephews, his own readings and studies, and the observation of the events of the war as they passed round him at a distance, are his only known occupations."

Did Milton marry?

Marriage—May-June, 1643. Milton marries Mary Powell, 17 years old, but she leaves him two months later. [Hanford believes this was 1642, as hostilities were breaking out, and the separation was political, not romantic]

Wife not a stranger—Masson: "Mary Powell in her childhood may not have been quite a stranger to him."

Returns a married man—Edward Phillips: "About Whitsuntide it was, or a little after, that he took a Journey into the Country; no body about him certainly knowing the Reason.... After a Month's stay, home he returns a Married-man, that went out a Batchelor; his Wife being Mary, the Eldest Daughter of Mr. Richard Powell, then a Justice of Peace of Forrest-hil, near Shotover in Oxfordshire."

Last place on earth—Masson: "Of all places in the world Forest Hill was the last where anybody that knew him would have expected to hear of his spending it.... Even with a pass, for Milton to venture into the neighbourhood of Oxford [the King's headquarters]—Milton, the Anti-Episcopal pamphleteer, and altogether one of the most marked of extreme Parliamentarians out of Parliament: why, it was venturing into the camp of the Philistines!"

No wife—Edward Phillips: "Michaelmas being come, and new news of his Wife's return, he sent for her by Letter.... A Messenger came back ... [and] reported that he was dismissed with some sort of Contempt. This proceeding, in all probability, was grounded upon no other Cause but this, namely, that the Family being generally addicted to the Cavalier Party, as they called it ... they began to repent them of having Matched the Eldest Daughter of the Family to a Person so contrary to them in Opinion.... [Milton] thought it would be dishonourable ever to receive her again, after such a repulse; so that he forthwith prepared to Fortify himself with Arguments for such a Resolution, and accordingly wrote two Treatises, by which he undertook to maintain, That it was against Reason, (and the enjoynment of it not proveable by Scripture), for any Married Couple disagreeable Humour and Temper, or having an aversion to each other, to be forc'd to live yok'd together all their Days."

Divorce pamphlet—August. Publication of *Doctrine and Discipline of Divorce*. This pamphlet in favor of liberalizing divorce brings Milton his first literary reputation—as a "libertine writer," calling for "divorce for pleasure"; he is called Milton the Divorcer for years afterward.

Forgiveness of wife—Edward Phillips: "On a sudden he was surprised to see one [his wife, Mary Powell] whom he thought to have never seen more, making Submission and begging Pardon on her Knees before him.... Partly his own generous nature ... and partly the strong intercession of Friends on both sides, soon brought him to an Act or Oblivion, and a firm League of Peace for the future."

What was he writing at this time?

1644, February. Second edition of *Doctrine and Discipline of Divorce*. Four editions in all, all unlicensed.

June. Pamphlet *Of Education : To Master Samuel Hartlib*.

July. *Judgment of Martin Bucer concerning Divorce*, a licensed publication. First signs of Milton's coming blindness.

Blindness—Toland: "His Blindness was rashly imputed by his Enemies to the avenging Judgment of God."

Clear to outward view—Richardson: The Colour of his Eyes inclin'd to Blue, not Deep; and though Sightless, they were as he says Himself, Clear to Outward View of Blemish or of Spot."

Milton pamphlets denounced—In August 1644, Milton's own books on divorce—one unlicensed, the other licensed—were denounced in a sermon delivered in Parliament.

November. *Areopagitica* published.

His particular province—John Phillips: "His next public work, and which seem'd to bee his particular Province, who was so jealous in promoting Knowlege, was *Areopagitica*."

Why did Milton use this title?

An imitation of a Greek classic.

Milton wrote *Areopagitica* in imitation of a classical model, Isocrates' Logos Areopagitikos, an argument addressed to the Athenian lawmakers. Isocrates was noted for bringing the rhetorical art of lawyers into the political arena. The title Milton uses is drawn from Isocrates, also—Areos pagos: hill of Ares or Mars Hill, site of the high court in Athens.

May be ironic—The obvious comparison with Isocrates' *Logos Areopagitikos* may be intended to be ironic, for in this book Isocrates argued for the reinstatement of the Court of the Areopagus, while Milton argues for unlicensed printing.

Not a speech—*Areopagitica* was one pamphlet among hundreds issued in the pamphlet wars in the absence of royal repression. The book is presented as a speech in which, from the beginning, Milton speaks directly to the parliamentarians. But this is simply a literary device, a pulpit to preach from; Milton did not deliver such a speech, nor was it entered into public record.

Milton's ironic title—Wittreich: "Through his title, Milton has, as it were, locked the ironic context and thus the full implications of his discourse from the members of Parliament who presumably would be unequipped to decipher the allusion. Milton's full meaning is reserved for the esoteric few who can read and comprehend. *Areopagitica* is at once a serious statement on the nature of liberty and a tour de force on Parliament, which Milton suspects, for all he says, is about to deny that liberty.... He envisions a regenerate England in the future, but the England of the present is not as yet regenerate."

Paul's speech—Some, such as E. Sirluck and M. Davis, have proposed that Paul's speech to the Athenians (Acts xvii, 18–34), an appeal for toleration, was the title reference.

Why did Milton write *Areopagitica*?

The 1643 Licensing Order.

He was protesting the English Parliament's *Licensing of Printing Order* of June 16, 1643, which was a repressive restatement of a 1641 law widely ignored. These parliamentary enactments came about to curb the explosion of diverse opinions, theories and outrageous libels that had spewed forth from print shops once the bishops and the King had been displaced from power. Royalists continued to protect the King—hostilities had broken out in the summer of 1642—but the King's ministers all had been stripped of power, and some put to death.

Commonplace book—Haller: He had long before concluded that men must be free to learn and to say and do what they thought would be well said and done. The tenor of the entries in the [Horton] commonplace book is plain. Milton was already thinking of the limitations that must be put on the interference of custom and government with the freedom of thought, utterance and action of men like himself. When in later years he looked back over his career, it would seem to him that for such freedom he had been contending all his life."

Personal reason—Milton also had a personal reason to write a defense of freedom of the press. In August 1644, Milton's own pamphlets in favor of loosening divorce laws—one unlicensed, the other licensed—were denounced in a sermon delivered in Parliament.

Main beliefs—Tillyard: "Milton's main beliefs at the time of *Areopagitica* may be outlined as follows. Man is born with the seeds of good and evil in him: mere environment cannot determine his character: in the most favourable environment evil might come out. But man has the power of choice, and knowing both good and evil it is possible for him to choose good. The present world may not ever be perfect, but it may be very much better. It is reasonable to have very high hopes; and it still seems likely that, in spite of set-backs, some great good is to happen to England in the immediate future. There is therefore every incentive for the noblest and most strenuous action."

After Italy—Milton: "I returned to my native country, after an absence of one year and about three months, at the time when Charles, having broken the peace, was renewing what is called the episcopal war with the Scots.... As soon as I was able I hired a spacious house in the city, for myself and my books; where I again, with rapture, resumed my literary pursuits....The vigour of the Parliament had begun to humble the pride of the bishops. As long as the liberty of speech was no longer subject to control, all mouths began to be opened against the bishops.... This awakened all my attention and my zeal. I saw that a way was opening for the establishment of real liberty."

Real liberty—Milton: "When the bishops could no longer resist the multitude of their assailants, I had leisure to turn my thoughts to other subjects; to the promotion of real and substantial liberty, which is rather to be sought from within than from without; and whose existence depends, not so much on the terror of the sword as on sobriety of conduct and integrity of life."

Three liberties—Milton: "When, therefore, I perceived that there were three species of liberty which are essential to the happiness of social life—religious, domestic, and civil; and as I had already written concerning the first, and magistrates were strenuously active in obtaining the third, I determined to turn my attention to the second, or the domestic species.... They seemed to involve three material questions—the conditions of the conjugal tie, the education of children, and the free publications of the thoughts.... On this subject, therefore, I published some books.... I then discussed the principles of education ."

No restraints—Milton: "Lastly, I wrote my *Areopagitica* after the true Attic style, in order to deliver the press from the restraints with which it was encumbered; that the power of determining what was true and what was false, what ought to be published and what to be suppressed, might no longer be entrusted to a few illiterate and illiberal individuals, who refused their sanction to any work which contained views or sentiments at all above the level of the vulgar superstition."

Divorce pamphlet scandal—Hales: "Not the least amongst the innovating offenders was Milton himself. His Divorce treatises had greatly scandalized many who had exulted in his succour in the controversy with the bishops in 1641 and 1642. They were denounced from the pulpit in a sermon preached before the two Houses of Parliament in 1644, and shortly afterwards petitioned against by the Stationers' Company. Milton then had personal reaons for coming forward as the champion of unlicensed printing and, apart from these personal motives, he was well aware of the animosity his Divorce writings had aroused, for he speaks of 'the world of disesteem' in which he found himself."

A great poem Milton never wrote—Tillyard: "*Areopagitica* is Milton's chief song of hope: in it he has uttered most of the few surviving fragments of the epic which I have supposed him to have contemplated as the beginning of the struggle between Parliament and Royalists, the Song of Innocence that never got written. But in another way it shows a maturity of experience quite new in Milton: a definite development of ideas towards Paradise Lost. Although pieces of the Arthuriad may have got themselves expressed, it must have been about the time Milton wrote *Areopagitica* that he abandoned any idea of writing such a poem."

What was the public reaction to *Areopagitica?*

No immediate reaction is recorded.

No mention was made in the English press for several years after the publication of *Areopagitica*, although Milton's pamphleteering skills apparently impressed Parliamentary leaders, for his name was advanced five years later for an appointment that may have been created for him: Latin Secretary to Oliver Cromwell—to be a pamphleteer in the cause of the New Model Army.

Not punished—Parker: "The *Areopagitica* had no practical effect, but it was known.... The Council of State is certain to have read it before hiring their Latin Secretary.... Most significant is the fact that the author was not punished. Milton was always breaking rules, in a deliberate and meaningful, if sometimes paradoxical fashion.... It seems likely that some persons in authority had an eye on him from the start, regarding him as an eloquent enfant terrible, impractical but sincere, and not to be treated like an ordinary ink-stained fanatic. It is otherwise difficult to explain, not only his own claim to being a privileged author, but also his several escapes from official censure during the autumn of 1644 when both the Commons and Lords, acting under outside pressure, ordered him investigated."

What did the early critics say about Milton?

Completely unnoticed—Haller: "[*Areopagitica*] seems to have contributed nothing to Milton's contemporary reputation and influence.... *Areopagitica*, notwithstanding its author's divorce heresy, seems to have gone completely unnoticed. It appears incredible that Milton's great plea for freedom of the press should have failed of any mention whatever in the thousands of pages printed at the time and abounding in specific references to hundreds of other publications, but the present writer is constrained to report that after a protracted search he has failed to find a single one. Surely, if the appearance of *Areopagitica* were ever to be noted, it should have been by Prynne in that chapter of his Fresh Discovery, written according to Thomason's dating about six months after the publication of *Areopagitica*, and devoted to the recent attacks upon the printing ordinance. But Prynne assails Henry Robinson, Lilburne, and the anonymous tracts of Overton, completely ignoring Milton. In the light of these facts, we must dismiss the notion that *Areopagitica* had any appreciable effect on the situation in 1644."

Out like a candle—Winstanley: "John Milton's ... Fame is gone out like a Candle in a snuff, and his Memory will always Stink, which might have lived in honourable repute, had he not been a notorious Trayter, and most impiously and villanously bely'd that blessed Martyr, King Charles the First."

A name—Wood: "[He] did great matters to obtain a name and wealth."

Natural greatness—Richardson: Milton appears to have had a Natural Greatness, Warmth and Vigour of Mind, together with an Openness and Generosity, all which is True Magnanimity. This Blazes wherever he goes from One End of his Life to the Other.... As He was Fully persuaded he was Engag'd in the Cause of God, and of Liberty, he exerted every Nerve."

Why was England in turmoil in the 1640s?

After years of repressive measures by Charles I, the Long Parliament legislated freedom of religion and political liberties. In 1642, civil war broke out between the Royalists and the Parliament. By 1644, the tide of battle was beginning to turn in favor of Parliament.

Faithless Charles I—Macaulay: "Charles the First succeeded to the throne.... He was ... a zealous Arminian, and, though no Papist, liked a Papist much better than a Puritan.... Faithlessness was the chief cause of his disasters."

Commons vs. the King—Macaulay: "And now began that hazardous game on which were staked the destinies of the English people. It was played on the side of the House of Commons with keenness, but with admirable dexterity, coolness, and perseverance. ... They were resolved to place the King in such a situation that he must either conduct the administration in conformity with the wishes of his Parliament, or make outrageous attacks on the most sacred principles of the constitution. They accordingly doled out supplies to him very sparingly.... He dissolved his first Parliament, and levied taxes by his own authority. He convoked a second Parliament, and found it more intractable than the first.... The King called a third Parliament, and soon perceived that the opposition was stronger and fiercer than ever. He now determined on a change of tactics."

Petition of Right—Macaulay: "The King ratified, in the most

solemn manner, that celebrated law, which is known by the name of the Petition of Right, and which is the second great Charter of the liberties of England. By ratifying that law he bound himself never again to raise money without the consent of the Houses, never again to imprison any person, except in due course of law, and never again to subject his people to the jurisdiction of courts martial."

Violation of Petition of Rights—Macaulay: "From March 1629 to April 1640, the Houses were not convoked.... During that part of his reign, the provisions of the Petition of Right were violated by him, not occasionally, but constantly, and on system.... A large part of the revenue was raised without any legal authority ... and persons obnoxious to the government languished for years in prison.... From the time of his third Parliament he was his own prime minister."

Religious refugees—During the years of Stuart repression, Puritan expeditions to America, including the Mayflower, were matched by Lord Baltimore's enterprise to set up Maryland as a Catholic refuge in 1634.

Short Parliament convened—Charles was defeated by the Scots in the Bishops' War in 1639 at Berwick. When more hostilities threatened, Charles was out of funds, and forced to call another Parliament to finance his adventures. The Short Parliament (April-May 1640) refused him money unless grievances were addressed, and he dissolved it quickly. But his payments to the Scots required another Parliament, and this became the Long Parliament.

What did King Charles expect to achieve?

A plan called Thorough—Macaulay: "Thomas Wentworth [Earl of Strafford] ... of a cruel and imperious nature, was the [King's] counsellor most trusted in political and military affairs. He ... had formed a vast and deeply meditated scheme which nearly confounded even the able tactics of the statesmen by whom the House of Commons had been directed. To this scheme ... he gave the expressive name of Thorough. His object was to do in England all, and more than all, that Richelieu was doing in France; to make Charles a monarch as absolute as any on the Continent; to put the estates andthe personal liberty of the whole people at the disposal of the crown; to deprive the courts of law of all independent authority. ... This was his end.... He saw that there was one instrument, and only one, by which his vast and daring projects would be carried into execution. That instrument was a standing army."

Laud's inspections—Macaulay: "William Laud, Archbishop of Canterbury ... had departed farthest from the principles of the Reformation, and had drawn nearest to Rome.... Under his direction every corner of the realm was subjected to a constant and minute inspection. Every little congregation of separatists was tracked out and broken up. Even the devotions of private families could not escape the vigilance of his spies."

Scottish revolt—Macaulay: "At this crisis an act of insane bigotry suddenly changed the whole face of public affairs.... Charles and Laud determined to force on the Scots the English liturgy.... The first performance of the foreign ceremonies produced a riot. The riot rapidly became a revolution. Ambition, patriotism, fanaticism, were mingled in one headlong torrent. The whole nation was in arms. ...No resource was left but a Parliament; and in the spring of 1640 a Parliament was convoked.... As soon as the Commons showed a disposition to take into consideration the grievances under which the country had suffered during eleven years, the King dissolved the Parliament with every mark of displeasure.... Everything now depended on the event of the King's military operations against the Scots."

Parliament reconvened—Macaulay: "Without money, without credit, without authority even in his own camp, he yielded the pressure of necessity. The Houses were convoked; and the elections proved that, since the spring, the distrust and hatred with which the government was regarded had made fearful progress. In November 1640 met that renowned Parliament which, in spite of many errors and disasters, is justly entitled to the reverence and gratitude of all who, in any part of the world, enjoy the blessings of constitutional government."

What was the Long Parliament?

Root and branch petition—Masson: 11 Dec. 1640—"Whereas the government of Archbishops and Lord-Bishops ... hath proved prejudicial and very dangerous.... We therefore most humbly pray and beseech this Honourable Assembly ... that the said government, with all its dependencies, roots, and branches, may be abolished, and all laws in their behalf made void."

King's counselors deposed—Macaulay: "The Star Chamber, the High Commission, the Council of York were swept away.... On the chief ministers of the crown the vengeance of the nation was unsparingly wreaked. The Lord Keeper, the Primate, the Lord Lieutenant were impeached.... Laud was flung into the Tower. Strafford [Wentworth] was impeached, and at length put to death by act of attainder."

Two parties—Macaulay: "Under this apparent concord a great schism was latent; and when, in October 1641, the Parliament reassembled after a short recess, two hostile parties ... appeared confronting each other. During some years they were designated as Cavaliers and Roundheads. They were subsequently called Tories and Whigs."

Burst all bounds—Masson: "The pamphlets on the Church question that had been produced since Milton's last might be counted by scores, if not by hundreds. The great majority of them, like Mliton's own [On Reformation in England], were unregistered; for the press had burst all bounds of licensing, and could not be brought within those bounds again by any Parliamentary orders or threats.... But not ... any other of the hundred pamphleteers that were writing on the Church question, can have been felt as such a voice of power, wherever there were competent readers, as this all-daring 'Mr. John Milton.' Whoever reads the pamphlet even now, or indeed any other of those early pamphlets of Milton, has his mind thrown into the strongest tumult."

Charles attempts to seize Parliament—Macaulay: "The smothered rage of the [Northern] Irish broke forth into acts of fearful violence.... A great army must now be raised.... [Charles] accordingly, a few days after he had promised the chiefs of the constitutional Royalists that no step of importance should be taken without their knowledge ... sent the Attorney General to impeach Pym, Hollis, Hampden, and other members of the House of Commons of high treason at the bar of the House of Lords.... [Charles] went in person, accompanied by armed men, to seize the leaders of the opposition within the walls of Parliament. The attempt failed.... A sudden and violent revulsion of feeling, both in the parliament and in the country, followed.... He had broken faith ... with his own adherents.... During the night which followed the outrage the whole City of London was in arms.... [Charles] quitted London, never to return till the day of a terrible and memorable reckoning had arrived."

Civil war begins—Macaulay: "The Roundheads of 1642, being unable to change the dynasty, were compelled to take a direct course towards their end.... In August 1642 the sword was at length drawn; and soon, in almost every shire of the kingdom, two hostile factions appeared in arms against each other.... When the war had lasted a year, the advantage was decidedly with the Royalists.... But the King suffered the auspicious moment to pass away; and it never returned. In August 1643 he sate down before the city of Gloucester ... [But] the siege of Gloucester was raised."

How did Cromwell rise to prominence?

Root and branch—Macaulay: "And now a new and alarming class of symptoms began to appear.... The Independents ... conceived that every Christian congregation had, under Christ, supreme jurisdiction in things spiritual ... and that Popery, Prelacy, and Presbyterianism were merely three forms of one great apostasy. In politics the Independents were, to use th phrase of their time, root and branch men, or ... radicals. Not content with limiting the power of the monarch, they were desirous to erect a commonwealth on the ruins of the old English polity.... Before the war had lasted two years they became, not indeed the largest, but the most powerful faction in the country.... The soul of that party was Oliver Cromwell."

Cromwell's perception—Macaulay: "[Cromwell] saw precisely where the strength of the Royalists lay, and by what means alone that strength could be overpowered. He saw that it was necessary to reconstruct the army of the Parliament. He saw also that there were abundant and excellent materials for the purpose, materials less showy, indeed, but more solid, than those of which the gallant squadrons of the King were composed. It was necessary to look for recruits who were ... of decent station and grave character, fearing God and zealous for public liberty. With such men he filled his own regiment.... The events of the year 1644 fully proved the superiority of his abilities."

New Model Army—Macaulay: "These events produced the Self-denying Ordinance and the new model of the army.... Cromwell made haste to organize the whole army on the same principles on which he had organized his own regiment. As soon as this process was complete, the event of the war was decided.... At Naseby took place the first great encounter between the Royalists and the remodelled army of the Houses. The victory of the Roundheads was complete and decisive."

Turning point—The Battle of Marston Moor in July 1644 was the turning point for the Parliamentary forces, a decisive victory by Cromwell's New Model Army, the Scots, and Sir Thomas

Fairfax's Yorkshiremen against Prince Rupert and the Marquess of Newcastle. Charles's headquarters at Oxford was captured two years later.

How had the press been restricted?

Stationers' Company—In 1557 the Stationers' Company of London—97 printers and their apprentices—was granted the exclusive privilege of printing and publishing in Britain.

Star Chamber—On Elizabeth's accession to the throne, the power of licensing was put in various government hands, then ratified by the Star Chamber (so named from the Camera Stellata, or chamber with a ceiling of stars) in 1566.

Church licensing—In 1586, Oxford and Cambridge were licensed, and licensing power was put in the hands of the Archbishop of Canterbury and the Bishop of London. Over the next fifty years, private presses were regularly evading these restrictions.

1637 Decree—11 July, 1637, a detailed law was passed called "Decree of Star-Chamber Concerning Printing": "No person or persons whatsoever shall presume to print, or cause to be printed ... any seditious, schismatical, or offensive Books or Pamphlets ... nor shall import any such Book or Books, nor sell or dispose of them, or any of them, nor cause any such to be bound, stitched, or sewed." Books and pamphlets "shall be first lawfully licenced and authorized ... and shall be also first entered into the Register's Book of the Company of Stationers," with 33 clauses in all.

Decree overthrown—The Long Parliament suppressed the Star Chamber in July 1641, and with it went all control over printing, including the detailed 1637 Order to license printing.

Protecting copyright—In January 29, 1642, the House of Commons issued an Order to reduce piracy and protect author's copyright, an endeavor that Milton approved: "It is ordered that the Master and Wardens of the Company of Stationers shall be required to take especial order, that the Printers do neither print, nor reprint anything without the name and consent of the Author: And that if any Printer shall notwithstanding print or reprint anything without the consent and name of the Author, that he shall then be proceeded against, as both Printer and Author thereof, and their names to be certified to this House."

1642 regulation on printing—9 March 1642, Commons issued an Order for regulating printing by a Committee for Examinations, which shall "have power to ... search in any house or place where there is just cause of suspicion, that presses are kept and employed in the printing of scandalous and lying pamphlets, and that they do demolish and take away such presses and their materials ... and bring the master-printers, and workmen printers before the said Committee." Further interim measures were issued in August 1642 and March 1643.

1643 tougher regulation—June 14, 1643, Parliament found that previous laws "have taken little or no effect.... Very many, as well Stationers and printers, as others of sundry other professions not free of the Stationers Company, have taken upon them to set up sundry private printing presses in corners, and to print, vend, publish and disperse books, pamphlets and papers, in such multitudes, that no industry could be sufficient to discover or bring to punishment, all the several abounding delinquents." Consequently, Parliament issued a further repressive order for the "Regulation of printing and for suppressing the great late abuses and frequent disorders in Printing many false, scandalous, seditious, libellous, and unlicensed pamphlets, to the great defamation of religion and government... Also authorizing the masters and wardens of the Company of Stationers to make diligent search, seize and carry away all such books as they shall find printed, or reprinted by any man having no lawful interest in them, being entered into the Hall Book to any other man as his proper copies [i.e., copyright]."

What points does Milton make in *Areopagitica*?

Need for copyright, but not other restrictions.

In arguing against the Order to regulate printing, Milton quickly affirms the necessity for copyright, but argues that licensing of printing is bad because:

1. Previous censors were repressive enemies of independent thought, such as the Inquisition.

2. In the nature of reading, even bad books may serve a lesson.

3. Bad books can't be suppressed by any law.

4. Freedom of thought will be discouraged.

Books are alive—Milton says that books are alive, and represent the better part of a person. The ancients banned books for two reasons—blasphemy and libel. Christian Rome added heresy to the list, and by 800 ce were making lists of books forbidden to read. By the 1400s, certain books—not just heretical ones—were forbidden to be printed, and finally all books were required to be licensed by the Church.

Glorious future—Milton's conclusion is that the Reformation in England has set in motion a glorious future for thought and freedoms.

Who states the other side of the argument?

Modern dictators seek total political control, and even a democracy when at war requires suppression of some ideas or points of view. Restricting freedom of the press is the easiest way to achieve that.

The Areopagi—Bishop Hall: "The Areopagi! Who were these? Truly, my masters, I had thought this had been the name of the place, not of the men."

Poets banished—Plato banishes poets from his Republic. Lenin's and Stalin's support for socialist realism made art and literature simply political means of education by the state.

Philosophical basis—Up to the time of his writing, no one had sought to describe the philosophical basis unconsciously shared by Puritans, Presbyterians, freethinkers, and all kinds of people with totally different ideas or religious beliefs. Milton clearly saw that a constitutional state, such as the one proposed in the Long Parliament, could not use the same methods that a monarch might without running the risk of creating a dictatorship similar to a monarchy.

What is special about printing?

The printing revolution released millions from the monopoly on reading and writing that had belonged to the Catholic Church. The ideas of the Reformation spread quickly through the printing of pamphlets. Printing created the general public and public opinion.

Benedictine scriptoria—Before the invention of printing, the Roman Catholic Church especially the Benedictine monasteries, had preserved learning from disappearing entirely in Europe through centuries of the Dark Ages, a time of economic collapse, downfall of the Roman Empire, decay of cities, trade, and travel.

Rural life was all that remained; land and the inheritance of land was the basis of all wealth. During this time, in Benedictine scriptoria, or writing rooms, teams of scribes copied out books by hand. Only monks and a few of the noble families with private libraries had books or knew how to read.

Mind control—This situation resulted in de facto control by the Catholic Church over people's minds, as long as no one protested or questioned the authority of the priest or the Church or the Latin Bible. But then in the 1440s and later, Johannes Gutenberg refined a system that required casting individual pieces of movable type from lead, a cheap supply of paper, inkballs, and a press that could deliver uniform intense pressure over a large area. The most important thing about printing is that it could not be contained by smashing presses; even an apprentice printer knew how it was done, and they could build the presses themselves.

Imitation manuscripts—At first, printing was considered a cheap imitation of scribing plain books, and printed books were certainly no comparison with the magnificent illustrated books of the scribes, sometimes inlaid with gold.

Reformation ideas—But the printing revolution released millions from the monopoly on reading and writing that had belonged to the Catholic Church. The ideas of the Reformation, reformers who wanted to change the Roman Catholic Church, spread quickly through the printing of pamphlets. An important thrust of the Spanish Inquisition was to throttle printing, thereby controlling the channels of information.

New ideas—Protestants soon discovered that their new ideas were not all the same, although each point of view was held with zealotry, especially the religious ideas, since they no longer relied on the authority of the Roman Pope. Pamphlet wars ensued on all kinds of issues, as an extension of the Medieval practice of public letters—that is, with no postal service, letters were passed from hand to hand as they went abroad, and each hand they passed through gained the knowledge of what was in the letter. Erasmus of Rotterdam was one scholar who used this technique with great effect, and then turned to printers to help him spread his ideas or suggestions on a much wider scale. Luther's first emergence on the stage of history was to nail his Ninety-Five Theses to the door of a church in Wittenberg, but he quickly found printing was an effective weapon in a war of ideas.

Unregulated—The question of regulating printing didn't come up in the beginning, because printing was seen simply as a technique that competed with the Benedictines and the private scribes that students and scholars of the new universities had to hire in order to duplicate the books found in private libraries.

Apprentice printers—The early German printers and their apprentices soon traveled to Italy, Spain, France, the Low Countries, England with their knowledge and skills. They built wooden presses braced against the ceiling and poured the lead for type and found ready customers everywhere they went—nobles jealous of other nobles' libraries, faculties, anyone who could read.

The first newspapers—The Church had its Inquisition, and governments had their laws. In the somnolent days before even the semblance of a newspaper or magazine had appeared, people got their news by rumor, by folk-song, by proclamation, or by informers. Among the first newsletters in England were printed letters of travelers in the Netherlands, eagerly read by investors who needed to know the events of war or foreign relations before other people knew. By 1621, N.B. (Nathaniel Butter or Nicholas Bourne) produced the Corante, or Weekely Newes from Italy, Germany, Hungarie, Spaine and France, the first regular English serial publication. Is it any surprise that Milton's *Areopagitica*, only twenty-three years later, would tackle the issue of freedom of the press?

How many people could read?

Estimates of literacy at this time vary from 1% to 50%.

Book production—Raymond Williams: "There is some evidence [before printing] of books being sold outside the monasteries and, later, outside the universities, which joined the monasteries in production. Certainly, in the fourteenth and fifteenth centuries, before the introduction of printing, manuscript books were being sold by dealers at fairs, by pedlars, and in London by shopkeepers, principally grocers and mercers. It seems fair to conclude that the largely professional reading public, of the clergy, of scholars and students, of doctors and lawyers, grew steadily throughout the Middle Ages, and that they were joined, in the later centuries, by a small but significant number of general readers."

Reading public—Williams: "The popularity of the chapbook, the jest-book, the ballad and the broadsheet dates at least from the sixteenth century, and this presupposes a reading public,

70

however small and irregular, of a general kind. Estimates of literacy at this time vary from the more than 50% implied by More ('farre more than fowre partes of all the whole divided into tenne coulde never reade englishe yet') to Gardiner's 'not the hundredth part of the realme.' "

Is freedom of the press the same as freedom of speech?

One person speaking to another is similar to, but is not the same as, one person speaking to millions.

Industry of jobs—Freedom of the press is based on the concept of free speech, but since the press is integrated into the social fabric of society as a communication network, an industry of jobs with tremendous cash flow, the source of education, entertainment, political propaganda, information, news, and culture, it is considered normal that restrictions and regulations and protocols for the press abound.

Proliferation of media—"The press" also continues to expand into new venues—faxes, CDs, interactive games, email, cable or wireless or satellite dish TV services are just a few recent additions to the press. Does Milton's argument apply to these?

Is freedom of the press a dead issue?

It becomes an issue whenever people are deprived of the free exchange of ideas.

Right or privilege—The U.S. Constitution makes it a right for Americans, but in much of the world, such a freedom is a privilege derived from governmental power.

Technologies—New technologies or situations always pose new problems for this issue. For example, 900 phone numbers, locked TV channels, violence on TV, new media.

Intellectual property—Even Milton recognized the necessity of protecting intellectual property with copyright protection for authors, as stated in the Long Parliament's original decree of January 1642.

What books were in Milton's library?

James Holly Hanford has researcheded all the references Milton used in his writings, in order to get a glimpse of the books in Milton's personal library. The list below is culled from Hanford's list to include books up to 1644, the date of publication of *Areopagitica.* We should not be surprised that the ancients are well represented here.

Lodovico Ariosto, *Orlando Furioso*

Aristotle, *Ethics*

Roger Ascham, *Toxophilus* [Archery]

Francis Bacon, *A Discourse of Church Affairs*

St. Basil, *Homiliae* [Homilies]

Venerable Bede, *Historia Ecclesiastica* [History of the Church]

Berni, *Orlando Inamorato Rifatto* [Orlando in Love Revisited]

Giovanni Boccaccio, *Vita di Dante* [Life of Dante]

Traiano Boccalini, *De' Ragguagli di Parnasso* [On Comparison of Poets]

Jean Bodin, *De Republica* [On the Republic]

Julius Caesar, *Commentaries*

William Camden, *Annales Rerum Anglicarum et Hibernicarum Regnante Elizabetha* [Annals of England and Ireland during the Reign of Elizabeth]

Edmund St. Campion, *History of Ireland*

John VI Cantacuzenus, *Historia Byzantina* [History of the Byzantine Empire]

Cedrenus, *Compendium Historiarum* [Encyclopedia of History]

Geoffrey Chaucer, *Canterbury Tales*

_____. *Romaunt of the Rose*

John St. Chrysostom, *In Genesim Homiliae* [Homilies in Constellations]

Clement of Alexandria, *Paedagogus* [Education]

_____. *Stromata* [Beds]

George Codinus (Curopalata), *De Officiis Magnae Ecclesiae et Aulae Constantinopolitanae* [On the Duty of the Great Church and Court of Constantinople]

Philippe de Comines, *Memoires* [Memoirs]

Cuspianus, *De Caesaris atque Imperiatoribus Romanis* [On the Caesars and the Roman Empire]

St. Cyprian, Bishop of Carthage, *De Singularitate*

Clericorum [On the Uniqueness of the Clergy]

_____. *De Spectaculis* [Of Shows]

_____. *Epistolae* [Letters]

_____. *Tractatus de Disciplina et Habitu Virginum* [Treatise on the Instruction and Keeping of Maidens]

Dante Alighieri, *Divinia Comedia* [Divine Comedy]

Andre DuChesne, *Histoire Generale d'Angleterre, d'Ecosse, et d'Irlande* [General History of England, Scotland and Ireland]

Eusebius, Bishop of Caesarea, *Historia Ecclesiastica* [History of the Church]

_____. *Vita Constantini* [Life of Constantine]

Evagrius Scholasticus, *Historia Ecclesiastica* [History of the Church]

Sextus Julius Frontinus, *Strategmata* [Strategies]

Gildas, *De Excidio Britanniae* [Of the Awakening of Britain]

Gilles, *Histoire des Eglises Vaudoises* [History of the Waldensians]

Bernard Girard, Sieur du Haillan, *L'Histoire de France* [History of France]

John Gower, *Confessio Amantis* [Confession of a Lover]

Gregoras Nicephoras, *Historia Byzantina* [History of the Byzantine Empire]

Gregory of Nyssa, *De Virginitate* [On Virginity]

Francesco Guicciardini, *Historia D'Italia* [History of Italy]

John Guillim, *A Display of Heraldry*

Hardyng, *Chronicle*

Hayward, *The Life and Reign of King Edward the Sixth*

Historia Miscella [Miscellaneous History]

Historia Scoticorum [History of the Scots]

Rafael Holinshed, *Chronicles of England, Scotland, and Ireland*

St. Ignatius, Bishop of Antioch, *Epistolae* [Letters]

Jovius (Paolo Giovio), *Historia sui Temporis* [History of Our Times]

Justinian, *Institutiones Juris Civilis* [Civil Law Education]

Justin Martyr, *Apologia pro Christianis* [Apology for Christianity]

_____. *Tryphon*

Lactantius, *De Ira Dei* [Of the Wrath of God]

_____. *De Opificio Dei* [Of God the Creator]

_____. *Diviniae Institutiones* [Divine Education]

William Lambarde, *Archeion, or a Commentary upon the High Courts of Justice in England*

Johannes Leunclavius, *Jus Graeco-Romanum* [Greek and Roman Law]

Niccolo Machiavelli, *Arte della Guerra* [The Art of War]

Peter Martyr (Pietro Martire of Vermigli), *In Librum Judicum* [On the Book of Judges]

Procopius, *De Bello Persico* [Of the Persian War]

Prudentius, *Liber Peristephanon* [Book about Stephan]

Samuel Purchas, *Pilgrimes*

Walter Raleigh, *History of the World*

Rivetus (André Rivet), *Praelectiones in Exodum* [Lectures on Exodus]

Sarpi (Paolo Servita), *Istoria del concilio Tridentino* [History of the Council of Trent]

Girolamo Savonarola, *Tratto delle Revelatione della Reformatione della Chiesa* [Treatise on the Revelation of the Reformation of the Church]

Schickhard, *Jus Regium Hebraeorum* [Law in the Kingdom of the Jews]

John Selden, *De Jure Naturali et Gentium juxta Disciplinam Hebraeorum* [On Natural Law and Peoples According to the Hebrew Instruction]

_____. *Uxor Ebraica* [Hebrew Marriage]

Sesellius (Claude de Seysel), *De Monarchia Franciae* [On French Monarchy]

Philip Sidney, *Arcadia*

Sigonius, *De Occidentali Imperio* [Of the Western Roman Empire]

_____. *De Regno Italiae* [Of the Italian Kingdom]

Sinibaldus (Joannes Benedictus), *Geneanthropeia* [Origin of Humanity]

Johannes Sleidanus, *De Statu Religionis et Reipublica Carolo Quinto Caesare* [On the State of Religion and the Republic of Charles the Fifth]

Socrates Scholasticus, *Historia Ecclesiastica* [History of the Church]

Sozomen, *Historia Ecclesiastica* [History of the Church]

Sir Thomas Smith, *Commonwealth of England*

John Speed, *History of Great Britain*

Clement Spelman, *Concilia, Decreta etc....in Re Eccleisastica Orbis Britanniae* [Councils, Decrees, etc....in the British Church World]

Edmund Spenser, *A View of the State of Ireland*

John Stow, *Annales, or a General Chronicle of England*

Sulpicius Severus, *Historia Sacra* [Sacred History]

Torquato Tasso, *Gerusalemme Liberata* [Jerusalem Liberated]

Alessandro Tassoni, *Pensieri* [Thoughts]

Tertullian, *Apologetica* [Apologetics]

_____. *De Jejuniis* [On Fasting]

_____. *De Spectaculis* [Of Shows]

Theodoretus, Bishop of Cyrrhus, *Historia Ecclesiastica* [Church History]

Thomasinus Paduanus, *Vita Petrarchi* [Life of Petrarch]

Thuanus (Jacques Auguste de Thou), *Historia sui Temporis* [History of Our Time]

Gabriele Villani, *Chroniche di Firenze* [Chronicles of Florence]

Von Herberstein (Sigismund), *Rerum Moscoviticarum Commentarii* [Commentary on Muscovite Matters]

Robert Ward, *Animadversions of Warre, or a Military Magazine of Rules and Instructions for the Managing of Warre*

William of Malmesbury, *De Gestis Regum Anglicorum* [On the Burden of the English Kingdom]

Is Milton's prose style remarkable?

Periodic style—Hales: "Milton is the last great writer in the old periodic style. No greater change came over our poetry than over our prose in the latter half of the seventeenth century."

Impassioned harangues—Lowell: "[Milton's prose works] are indeed for the most part the impassioned harangues of a supremely eloquent man, full of matter, but careless of the form in which he utters it, rich in learning, but too intent on the constant display of it with the cumbrous prodigality of one to whom such wealth is new.... He surely, if any, was what he calls 'a mint-master of language.' ... He is not so truly a writer of great prose, as a great man writing in prose, and it is really Milton that we seek there more than anything else."

Greatest prose work—Read: "The *Areopagitica* is Milton's greatest prose work, and this rank is given to it on account of its inherent qualities of fervour and style: but it is great also because of its wisdom, its logic and the universal application of its argument. Every newly established tyranny brings its pages to life again: there is no encroachment on 'the liberty to know, to utter and to argue freely' which it does not anticipate and oppose with unanswerable reason."

What do modern critics say about Milton?

Natural hierarchy—Wittreich: "Despite the obvious tactical differences...both orators are trying to avert anarchy and preserve democracy. Milton and Isocrates, moreover, share a belief in a natural hierarchy and apprehend the truth afforded to them by experience, namely that when those best fit to rule are not ruling, or are not ruling well, democracy becomes tyranny."

To indite a pamphlet—Lowell: "During the hurly-burly of the English Civil War, which made the bee in every man's bonnet buzz all the more persistently to be let forth, whoever would now write to his newspaper was driven, for want of that safety-valve, to indite a pamphlet, and, as he believed that the fate of what for the moment was deemed the Universe hung on his opinion, was eager to make it public ere the opportune moment should be gone by forever."

Uncurtailed utterance—Lowell: "All these sects, since each singly was in a helpless and often hateful minority, were united in the assertion of their right to freedom of opinion and to the uncurtailed utterance of whatever they fancied that opinion to be. Many of them, it should seem, could hardly fail in their mental vagabondage to stumble upon the principle of universal toleration, but none discovered anything more novel than that Liberty of Prophesying is good for Me and very bad for Thee."

Education preserves liberty—Wittreich: "For Milton and Isocrates ... education is tantamount to attaining and preserving real liberty. ... Isocrates and Milton attribute to the educated man the capacity for distinguishing between good and evil and the perspicuity for selecting the former."

Masculine energy—Haller: "More than any other English poet Milton may be said to express the moral energy of his race. He presents the soul of his people in its most masculine phase, not as it has turned aside to love, nature or religion for escape, consolation or rapture, but as it has wreaked its energies on the ruling of men and the making of laws.... It has proved impossible for most of his readers to judge him without personal feeling."

Right use of freedom—Lowell: "Parliament in June, 1643, passed an Ordinance to restrain unlicensed printing. They had so little learned how to use their newly acquired freedom as to be certain that they could compel other men to the right use of theirs. This is not to be wondered at, for even democracies are a great while in finding out that everything may be left to the instincts of a free people save those instincts themselves, and that these, docile if guided gently, grow mutinous under unskillful driving."

Unwise repression—Lowell: "Unwise repression made evasion only the more actively ingenious, and gave it that color of righteousness which is the most dangerous consequence of ill-considered legislation."

Poet and Puritan—Haller: "Milton has always seemed to many something of an enigma. What should he, the great artist and apostle of freedom, be doing among the Philistines? How could it be that he should be an exception to the rule stated by Matthew Arnold that great English poetry is written only by members of the established church? Over this paradox successive critics have boggled. Some have acknowledged Milton's genius while deploring his morals and his political opinions. Others have admired him but not entirely for the things he himself most esteemed.... He was ... a man somehow at war with himself, the poet and the Puritan."

Enough to shatter any government—Lowell: "Every doctrine inconceivable by instructed men was preached, and the ghosts of every dead and buried heresy did squeak and gibber in the London streets. The right of private misjudgment had been exercised so fantastically on the Scriptures that thoughtful persons were beginning to surmise whether there were not enough explosive material between their covers to shatter any system of government or of society that ever was or will be contrived by man. All this was the natural result of circumstances wholly novel, of a universal ferment of thought or of its so many plausible substitutes, enthusiasm, fanaticism, monomania, and every form of mental and moral bewilderment suddenly loosed from the unconscious restraints of traditional order.... It was a state of things that should have been left to subside, as it had arisen, through natural causes, but the powers that be always think themselves wiser than the laws of Nature or the axioms of experience.

Stationers'—Lowell: "As respects the Stationers' Company, [Milton] should have complied with the law, since entry in their register was the only security for copyright, and he believed, as he tells us in his *Eikonoclastes*, that 'every author should have the property in his work reserved to him after death as well as living.' It was the infringement of piratical printers during the general confusion which seems first to have moved the Stationers' Company to protest."

Universal tolerance—Lowell: "There is in [*Areopagitica*] implicitly the doctrine of universal toleration."

Champion of freedom—Lowell: "Milton was always a champion of freedom as he understood it ... but in truth no man was ever farther from being a democrat in the modern sense than he. The government that he preferred would have been that of a Council chosen by a strictly limited body of constituents and this indirectly...something like a Venetian Republic without a Doge.... For the 'rude multitude' as he calls it, he had an unqualified contempt."

Unbounded or bound liberty—Johnson: "The danger of such unbounded liberty, and the danger of bounding it, have produced a problem in the science of government which human understanding seems hitherto unable to solve. If nothing may be published but what civil authority shall have previously approved, power must always be the standard of truth; if every dreamer of innovations may propagate his projects, there can be no settlement; if every murmurer at government may diffuse discontent, there can be no peace; and if every sceptic in theology may teach his follies, there can be no religion. The remedy against these evils is to punish the authors; for it is yet allowed that every society may punish, though not prevent, the publication of opinions, which that society shall think pernicious; but this punishment, though it may crush the author, promotes the book; and it seems not more reasonable to leave the right of printing unrestrained, because writers may be afterwards censured, than it would be to sleep with doors unbolted, because by our laws we can hang a thief."

Was Milton's argument borne out by history?

Milton as licenser—In 1649, Milton was appointed licenser of the journal Mercurius Politicus for two years, which he also helped to edit.

L'Estrange—In 1662, the post of Licenser was revived, and in the next year, Roger L'Estrange, a partisan pamphleteer, was appointed, and served quite actively until about 1688, when Fraser briefly held the post, but was dismissed after letting a book pass. Bohun was the last Licenser.

End of licensing—Printing was finally unlicensed in 1694, fifty years after Milton's essay. The 1643 Ordinance was modified in 1647, 1649 and 1652, although one Licensor, Gilbert Mabbott, resigned in 1649, apparently persuaded by *Areopagitica*. When power swung from the Presbyterian party to the Independents, the "root and branch" religionists, the Licensing law was not enforced. In 1662, the Restoration of the monarchy gave new life to the office of Licenser, although the Star Chamber was not revived.

Paradise Lost escaped—Under this Act of 1662, Milton's own works were questioned—*Paradise Lost* escaped the knife but not his *History of Britain*. The Act of 1662 expired in 1679, was renewed in 1685 until 1692, then renewed two more years. The question came up again in 1697, 1703 and 1713 without success.

After 50 years—It took fifty years, the 1690s, for England to abandon licensing for printing. In the United States, the trial of John Peter Zenger in 1735, argued by Andrew Hamilton, established the right of a jury, not a judge, to decide whether or not printed matter was in fact libellous. The first copyright law, the one area involving printing that Milton believed should be licensed, was passed in 1842 in Great Britain.

U.S. reluctance—The U.S. did not subscribe to international copyright conventions until 1893, acting on the testimony of Mark Twain and other American writers and publishers. Today proponents of democracy the world over rely on freedom of the press as well as freedom of discussion, freedom of movement, and other freedoms.

What was the publication history of *Areopagitica*?

1644, November. First publication of *Areopagitica*.

1679. A mutilated and plagiarized edition of *Areopagitica* entitled *A Just Vindication of Learning and the Liberty of the Press* by Philopatris (Charles Blount) published.

1693. An abridged edition of *Areopagitica* entitled Reasons humbly offered ... published.

1738. Second edition published of *Areopagitica*, with preface by James Thomson.

1772. Separate edition published of *Areopagitica*. Now popular, *Areopagitica* became a cornerstone of the Enlightenment and the American and French Revolutions.

1788. Mirabeau's *Sur la liberté de la Presse, imité de l'Anglois de Milton*, basically an adaptation of *Areopagitica*.

1792. Separate edition of *Areopagitica* published.

1819. Separate edition by T. Holt White of *Areopagitica*, the basis for later scholarly editions.

1866. Separate edition of *Areopagitica* by John W. Hales, with excellent notes.

1868. Edward Arber's edition of *Areopagitica* published in English Reprints Series.

1872. Calcutta edition of *Areopagitica* by Mr. Lobb, modernized for Indian readers.

What happened in Milton's later life?

1645. Mary Powell, his wife who ran away, reconciles with him. Eventually they have 4 children. *Tetrachordon* and *Colasterion* published, unlicensed. No prosecution for these publications.

1646–1648. No new publications for three years.

1649. January. *The Tenure of Kings and Magistrates* published two weeks after Charles was beheaded. October. *Eikonoklastes* (response to the Royalist Eikon Basilike), written on order of the Council of State.

1650, December. On commission from the Council of State, Milton answers the scholarly Claudius Salmasius's *Defensio Regia pro Carolo I* with the pamphlet that catapulted Milton to national attention, *Johannis Miltoni, Angli, pro Populo Anglicano Defensio*, later known as *Defensio Prima*. Both books had an international audience.

1652. Mary Powell, his first wife, dies. Six weeks later his son John dies at age two. Milton becomes totally blind, with three daughters to care for.

1654, May. The *Defensio Secunda* appears. Tillyard calls it the "greatest of Milton's prose works," but it is more of a defense of Milton than of Britain. This includes Milton's own account of writing *Areopagitica*. Salmasius had died in 1653 without replying, and Milton chose to attack a lesser writer, Morus. This, and a third, *Defensio pro Se* (1655), met with little response. This pamphlet war had been won.

1655. Milton is pensioned, released from most official duties. He returns to his *History of Britain* project.

1658. *Paradise Lost* begun. Cromwell dies.

1659. Milton begins a series of pamphlets advising the Parliament on how to achieve religious and civil reform.

1660. The Restoration puts an end to Milton's political career. He is free to write poetry again.

1663. *Paradise Lost* finished. Milton's third marriage.

1667 Publication of *Paradise Lost*.

1674, November 8. Death of John Milton.

BIBLIOGRAPHY

Arber, Edward, ed. *John Milton. Areopagitica Preceded by Illustrative Documents.* Philadelphia: Albert Saifer, 1972

Clyde, William W. *The Struggle for the Freedom of the Press from Caxton to Cromwell.* Oxford, 1934.

Cotterill, H.B., ed. *Areopagitica.* New York, 1904.

Darbishire, Helen. *The Early Lives of Milton.* London: Constable, 1932.

Davis, Michael, *Areopagitica and Of Education.* London: 1963

Diekhoff, John S. *Milton on Himself.* New York: Oxford University Press, 1939

Hales, John W. *Milton: Areopagitica,* Oxford: Oxford University Press, 1917

Hall, Bishop. *Defence of the Humble Remonstrance...*

Haller, William. *The Rise of Puritanism.* New York: Columbia University Press, 1938; rpt. New York: Harper & Row, 1957.

_____. *Tracts on Liberty in the Puritan Revolution, 1638–1647.* New York: Octagon Books, 1934. rpt. 1965.

Hanford, James Holly. *John Milton Poet and Humanist.* Cleveland: Press of Western Reserve University, 1966.

Hughes, Marritt Y. *John Milton: Prose Selections.* 1947

Hunter, William B., Jr. *A Milton Encyclopedia.* Lewisburg: Bucknell University Press, 1978

Jebb, Richard. *Areopagitica.* Cambridge, 1918.

Johnson, Samuel. *Lives of the English Poets,* London, 1781

Lowell, James Russell. *Areopagitica.* New York: The Grolier Club, 1890

Macaulay, Thomas Babington. *The History of England from the Accession of James the Second.* Leipzig: Bernhard Tauchnitz, 1849

Masson, David. *The Life of John Milton, Vol II 1638–1643.* New York: Peter Smith, 1946.

82

Parker, William Riley. *Milton's Contemporary Reputation,* rpt., Folcroft, Pa.: Folcroft Press, 1969

Edward Phillips (Milton's nephew): *The Life of Mr. John Milton,* 1694. In Darbishire, The Early Lives of Milton.

Phillips, John (Milton's nephew). *The Life of Mr. John Milton.* In Darbishire, The Early Lives of Milton.

Read, Herbert. "On Milton's *Areopagitica*," in *Adelphi* XXI (1944), 9–15.

Richardson, J. Sr. *Explanatory Notes and Remarks on Milton's Paradise Lost, With the Life of the Author.* London: James, John, and Paul Knapton, 1734.

Schreider, Theodore. *Free Speech Bibliography.* New York, 1922.

Sirluck, Ernest. *Complete Prose Works of John Milton,* ed. Don M. Wolfe et al. Vol. II. New Haven: Yale University Press, 1953–

Tillyard, E.M.W. *Milton,* London: Chatto & Windus, 1966.

Toland, John. *The Life of John Milton,* 1698.

Williams, Raymond. *The Long Revolution.* New York: Harper & Row, 1966.

Winstanley, William. *Lives of the most famous English Poets,* 1687.

Wittreich, Joseph Anthony, Jr. "Milton's *Areopagitica*: Its Isocratic and Ironic Contents," in *Milton Studies* IV, ed. James D. Simmonds, Pittsburgh: University of Pittsburgh Press, 1972.

Wood, Anthony à. *Fasti Oxonienses or Annals of the University of Oxford,* 1691.

a trivial and malignant encomium. From the religious pamphlet wars: Bishop Hall's (d. 1656) *A Modest Confutation of a Slanderous and Scurrilous Libel intituled Animadversions upon the Remonstrant's Defence against Smectymnuus* (1642) attacks Milton's 1641 pamphlet criticizing Bishop Hall's reply to Smectymnuus.

prelates and cabin counsellors that usurped of late. The Committee of Council, led by Archbishop Laud and the Earl of Strafford; also known as the Junto or the Cabinet.

him who from his private house wrote ... Isocrates in his *Λόγος Αρεοπαγίτικος* writes as if addressing the lawmakers of Athens, as Milton does in *Areopagitica. Ἄρεος πάγος*—hill of Ares (Mars), site of the high court in Athens.

wholly dedicated to studious labors. "wherein I have spent and tired out almost a whole youth," Milton reports in his *Apology for Smectymnuus.*

that part which preserves justly everyone's copy[right] to himself. A book registered with the Stationers' Company in the name of the printer or publisher could not be published without consent of the Stationers and of the owner of the "copy" (copyright), as specified in the Order of Parliament of June 14, 1643.

quadragesimal and matrimonial when the prelates expired. Quadragesimal is to be excused from fasting at Lent; this and a church marriage license were no longer required during Commonwealth times. The bishops were ejected (expired) from the House of Peers early in 1641, though Episcopacy was not abolished until October 9, 1646.

discourse. Protagoras, Truth, or concerning the Real (Diogenes Laertius IX, 51).

Lycurgus ... Homer. According to Aelian, *Varia Historia*, XIII, 14.

Thales. This is a doubtful story: Thaletas lived a hundred years later than Lycurgus.

women were all unchaste. Spartan women were not restricted to household activities, but were athletic and openly public.

Carneades, Critolaus, Diogenes. These three Greeks had come in 155 bce to argue a case on behalf of Athens at the Roman Senate. See glossary for particulars. Young Romans who knew Greek were enthralled by Carneades' lectures on justice, in which he refutes himself, so much so that it created a scandal. Cato led the Senate in dismissing their case, but Greek philosophy later came to dominate Roman thinking.

Sabine austerity ... fell to the study. Cato would often retreat to his father's farm in the Sabine territory, living as frugally as his rural neighbors. At age eighty, he undertook the study of his bugaboo, Greek literature.

libels were burnt. The eighth of the Twelve Tables dealt with libel.

little else but tyranny. Milton here skips three hundred years to Constantine (ruled 306–337 ce).

general councils. Ecumenical (world-representing) council, the first of which met at Nicaea in Bithynia in 325 ce, at which the Nicene Creed was issued.

about the year 400. Fourth Council of Carthage, 398 ce.

prohibition ... purgatory. The Index Librorum Prohibitorum and the Index Expurgatorius.

St. Peter ... the keys. Matthew XVI, 18–19.

Suetonius. Wherever I would come to a banquet, someone would send out a wind and a noise from his belly.

Lambeth House ... west end of Paul's. Residences of the Archbishop of Canterbury and the Bishop of London. The Star Chamber order of 1586 established these two as licensors of all books. In 1637, law, history and heraldry books were given other licensors.

our English. In his youth, Milton was well on his way to becoming a European poet with brilliant Latin poetry. But in The Reason of Church Government (1641), he admits to the ambition to be a national poet: "I applied myself to that resolution which Ariosto followed ... to fix all the industry and art I could unite to the adorning of my native tongue ... not caring to be once named abroad, though perhaps I could attain to that, but content with these British Islands as my world."

no envious Juno. Alcmena in labor cried out for her maid, but Hera forced the maid to sit cross-legged at the door. Another maid made her think that Alcmena had given birth, and in the moment she uncrossed her legs, Alcmena gave birth to Hercules.

mysterious iniquity. Reformers identifed the Church of Rome with the woman named Mystery, mother of harlots and abominations of the earth. (Revelation, XVII, 5).

new limbos and new hells. Limbus—fringe, border. On the outskirts of hell, the Roman Catholic Church declared the Limbus Patrum for those just persons who had died before Christ and the Limbus Infantium (or Limbus puerorum) for infants who died in original sin. Another region rumored to exist was the Limbus Fatuorum, or Paradise of Fools.

Paul ... three Greek poets. Aratos (270 BCE) in Acts XVII, 28: "As certain also of your own poets have said, For we are also his offspring." Euripides in I Corinthians, XV, 33: "Evil communications corrupt good manners." Epimenides of Crete (600 bce) in Titus I, 12: "The Cretans are always liars ..."

seven liberal sciences. In medieval studies grammar, logic and rhetoric form the Trivium, and arithmetic, geometry, astronomy and music the Quadrivium.

that of the Apostle. I Thessalonians V, 21.

another remarkable saying. Titus I, 15.

Ephesian books. Acts XIX, 19.

wayfaring. The first edition has wayfaring, the quarto edition warfaring. Whether Milton approved or suggested the change is in debate.

I name not him. Probably Skelton (actually a Rector of Diss in Norfolk), or Wolsey, or Thomas Cromwell, or Andrew Borde, or a man named Gray.

by the north of Cathay eastward. Referring to the longtime quest for the Northwest Passage.

prophecy of Isaiah. Acts VIII, 30.

exploit ... pound up. An attempt in Borrowdale to keep in the cuckoo with a wall to make the spring last forever.

judgment of Aristotle ... Solomon ... our Saviour. See Ethics I, 3. Proverbs XVII, 7 and XXVI, 5. Matthew VII, 6.

regulate all recreations. A rhetorical extension of Archbishop of Canterbury Laud's plan for every bishop to censor every lecturer, listed in Articles of Visitation.

our garments also. Regulations on dress materials were common at the end of the Middle Ages, such as the Statute of Apparel, 1363, and into Tudor times.

mixed conversation. Puritans did not approve of mixed dancing.

Plato there mentions. Republic, IV.

many sects refusing books. Such as the Druids, early Cabalists, and the Waldenses (Vaudois).

patriarchal licenser. Bishop Laud was rumored to wish to become the Patriarch of the Western Church, equal to the Patriarchs of Rome, Jerusalem, Antioch, and Alexandria.

what an author this violence. Probably Sir Edward Coke, parts of whose posthumous Institutes were published "with some disadvantage" according to Prynne.

monopolized … tickets and statutes and standards. Monopolies even of common necessities greatly abused their privileges in the 17th century. Tickets—credit chits; statutes—securities given for debts contracted; standards—weights and measures.

their learned ones. Jacob Gaddi, Carolo Dati, Frescobaldo of Florence are mentioned in Milton's Second Defence.

covenants and protestations. Covenant or League between England and Scotland (1643); the Protestation (1641) by Lords and Commons to maintain constitutional liberties.

obstructing violence. Harsh Star Chamber sentences on Leighton (1630), Prynne (1634 and 1637), and the Puritans Bastwick and Burton were met with indignation and public anger.

after the malmsey. Breakfast did not become a custom until the 18th century. Earlier English practice was to have a morning pint of ale and no food. Malmsey—sweet wine from Malvasia in Morea near Crete.

the Turk. Printing was not allowed in Turkey until the mid-eighteenth century. *Al-Koran*—the reading.

Egyptian Typhon. Plutarch in *On Isis and Osiris* associates Ἶσις with ἴσημι or knowledge, and Τυφῶν with τετυφωμένος—puffed up.

the Persian wisdom. Pliny the Elder in his Natural History suggests a connection with Britain, but does not state it as fact.

the old philosophy. The Druids were thought to believe in reincarnation, but the idea that Pythagoras received this idea from Britain is unsubstantiated.

first to his English. Milton believed that England was "chosen" to initiate the Reformation. In *Doctrine and Discipline of Divorce* (1643), he writes:

> It would not be the first or second time since our
> ancient Druids (by whom this island was the
> Cathedral of Philosophy to France) left off their pagan
> rites, that England has had this honor vouchsafed
> from Heaven to give out Reformation to the world.
> Who was it but our English Constantine that baptized
> the Roman Empire? Who but the Northumbrian
> Willibrode, and Winifride of Devon with their followers,
> were the first Apostles of Germany? Who but Alcuin
> and Wycliffe our countrymen opened the eyes of
> Europe, the one in Arts, the other in Religion? Let not
> England forget her precedence of teaching Nations
> how to live.

shop of war. In 1644, forces loyal to Parliament fought the battle of Marston Moor.

five months yet to harvest. Referring to the New Model Army.

bought that piece of ground. Livy (XXVI, ii) reports Hannibal's outrage:

> It was learned from a captive that during those days
> the very ground (as it happened) on which he himself
> was encamped had been sold without any depreciation
> of its value on that account. Now this seemed such
> haughtiness—such insolence—that a buyer should
> have been found at Rome for soil which he himself
> occupied and possessed by right of conquest—that he
> immediately summoned an auctioneer and ordered
> that the money-changers' shops, which then stood
> about the Roman Forum, should be sold.

I dispraise not. In his Second Defence, Milton excuses his nonparticipation in the army of Parliament by saying that he fought with other weapons.

as Micaiah. I Kings XXII, 1–28.

hand-writing nailed to the cross. Colossians II, 14.

that order published next before this. The Order of the Commons of Jan. 29, 1642, which ordered

> that the printers do neither print, nor reprint anything without the name and consent of the author: And that if any printer shall notwithstanding print or reprint anything without the consent and name of the author, that he shall then be proceeded against, as both printer and author thereof, and their names to be certified to this House.

authentic Spanish policy. Of the Spanish Inquisition.

fallen from the stars. Isaiah XIV, 12.

GLOSSARY

Academic: The Academy was Plato's school.

advertisement: Advice, instruction.

Aiakos: one of three judges of Hades.

airy burgomasters: Imaginary mayors or magistrates.

Alcmena: mother of Hercules.

Antisthenes: A Cynic philosopher, who believed in mind and scorned concern for the body or pleasure. Antisthenes once studied with Socrates.

Apollinaris and his son: The two Apollinarii overcame a ban on Hellenistic culture by Julian the Apostate (361–363), the father by rewriting grammar especially for Christians and translating the Old Testament into hexameters and every kind of Greek meter and form, including tragedy, and the son by reorganizing the Gospels and New Testament books into Platonic dialogues.

apophthegma: something said plainly.

apophthegms: *Laconic Apophthegms* is the title of a collection by Plutarch of Lacedaemonian proverbs.

Aquinas: Thomas Aquinas (c.1224–1274) philosopher; synthesized Aristotle's philosophy for the Catholic Church.

Aratos: (270 bce). Quoted by Paul in *Acts* XVII, 28: "As certain also of your own poets have said, For we are also his offspring."

Arcadia: The Countess of Pembroke's *Arcadia* (1590) apparently written by her brother, Sir Philip Sidney, edited by her after his death.

Archilochus: (714–676 BCE). Greek poet and satirist.

Areos Pagos: hill of Ares (Mars Hill), site of the high court in Athens.

ribald of Arezzo: Pietro Aretino (1492–1557) wrote burlesques and satires.

Aristippos: Disciple of Socrates, founded the Cyrenaic school. Aristippos taught the temperate use of pleasure: "To subdue circumstance to oneself, not oneself to circumstances."

Arminius: James Harmensen or Arminius, (1560–1609) was a Dutch theologian who was hired in 1588 to defend Beza's teaching of predestination against attack, but became convinced of the opposing viewpoint.

Atlantic: referring to *New Atlantis* by Francis Bacon, a utopian novel.

augur: Six Roman diviners interpreted the gods' messages in the flights of birds.

Bacon, Francis: Author of the Utopian piece *New Atlantis* (from Atlantis, or island of Atlas). He also wrote *An Advertisement touching the Controversies of the Church of England* (written 1589, published 1640).

baited down: As in bear-baiting, a popular English sport.

ballad: any type of song

Baltimore, Lord George Calvert: Colonizer in Ireland and America.

Basil the Great: (329–379). Bishop of Caesarea in Cappodocia, and founder of monasteries.

Bastwick: Puritan zealot, who attacked Laud and English bishops as enemies of God. He lost his ears and was exiled by Star Chamber decree.

beatific vision: Visio Beatifica—seeing God.

Birkenhead, Sir John: editor and chief writer of *Mercurius Aulicus*, a Royalist periodical (1642–1645).

Bourne, Nicholas: English publisher and printer.

Breviary: abridgement, compendium.

Lord Brooke: Robert Greville, Lord Brooke, an extreme Puritan and member of the House of Lords, was killed March 2, 1642 while leading the forces of Parliament at Lichfield. Milton refers to his Nov. 1641 pamphlet *A Discourse opening the nature of Episcopacy.*

Bucer, Martin: (1491–1551) Leading organizer in the Reformation in Strasbourg; author of *The Kingdom of Christ.* A refugee in 1549, Bucer was welcomed at Cambridge, where he lived until his death in 1551.

Bull: Bulla in Latin, an ornamental boss, later the wax seal attached to legal papers.

Butter, Nathaniel: English printer and publisher

Calvin: John Calvin (1509–1564), author of *Institutes* and Reformation leader.

canonical sleight: Apostolic Canons were late forgeries. Ecclesiastical canons were begun in 380, and canon law introduced by Gratian in 1151.

Caraffa: In 1543 Cardinal Caraffa ordered no book to be printed without license of the Inquisition, booksellers must send their catalogs to Rome. Thus was begun the *Index Expurgatorius.*

Carneades: Founder of the New Academy, a Skeptic philosophy. Carneades was born at Cyrene, and lived c.219-129 bce. On a trip with Critolaus and Diogenes the Babylonian to Rome in 155 bce to argue a case on behalf of Athens at the Roman Senate, Carneades created a scandal among young Romans by giving lectures and then refuting himself with rhetorical wizardry.

Castle St. Angelo: Castello S. Angelo near the Vatican in Rome.

Catena: series or "chain" of authorities.

Cathay: China. Milton here refers to the longtime quest for the Northwest Passage.

Cato the Censor: (234–149 bce) Marcus Porcius Cato, "Cato Major," was the first important Latin prose writer. He served as Censor in 184 bce, completely opposed to anything Greek, and led the Roman Senate in dismissing the case presented by Carneades, Critolaus and Diogenes the Babylonian, but Greek philosophy came to dominate Roman thinking. Even Cato in his old age began the study of Greek.

Catullus: Roman poet (87–47 BCE), famous for his invective.

cautelous: (Late Latin) deceitful.

Cavaliers: Englishmen in the Royalist cause, supporting Charles I.

censure: Opinion, not necessarily bad.

Charles I: Stuart king of England, whose authority was in question when Milton wrote *Areopagitica*.

chetiv: word as written; rather than edit holy books, rabbinical commentators supplied a correct or more appropriate word (*keri*—to be read) in the margin while leaving untouched the word as written in the text (*chetiv* or *cethib*).

chop: Exchange.

Chrysostom: John Chrysostom, Bishop of Constantinople (347–407).

Cicero: Roman Senator, a Stoic philosopher and orator. Jerome reports that after Lucretius' death, Cicero edited Lucretius' poem *De Rerum Natura* and published it, or republished it. Cicero is on record as lukewarm about the poem.

Clement: Clement of Alexandria's *Hortatory Address to the Greeks* dismissed polytheism.

Coat and conduct: county taxes from Henry VII's day, given to recruits to buy a white cassock with a red cross on it, and to travel to the training camp, much protested in petitions to Parliament in 1641.

Coke, Sir Edward: Secretary of State to Charles I from 1625 to 1639, most of the time Parliament was not convened. Parts of his posthumous *Institutes* were published "with some disadvantage" according to Prynne.

combust: In conjunction with, or less than 8.5 degrees from, the sun, thought to be "burnt."

Constance, Council of: (1414–1418) This Church council was called by John XXIII, one of three concurrent Popes, to resolve the Great Schism—eventually all three Popes were deposed, and Otto Colonna became Martin V, restoring the unity of the Catholic Church. Among other restrictive measures, the Council ordered Wycliffe's bones to be dug up and burned.

controversal faces: faces looking in opposite directions, as

Janus' faces.

conventicle: Small meeting or assembly, especially of noncomformists.

Old Convocation house: A convocation, or national assembling of clergy, was called by the Long Parliament in July 1643 at the Westminster Assembly, first in Henry VII's Chapel and then in the Jerusalem Chamber.

Copy: Copyright, the one regulation that Milton insisted should remain on printing.

criticisms of sin: Varieties of sin. Criticisms are things discriminated.

Critolaus: Head of the Peripatetic school, which had been founded by Aristotle.

Cromwell, Thomas: Leader of the Independent party in Parliament, who fashioned the New Model Army that crushed the Royalists; eventually Cromwell became Lord Protector, with Milton as his able Latin Secretary.

Danegelt: originally shipmoney levied in 1007 to build a navy against the Danes; Charles I levied it in 1634–36, but it was declared illegal in 1637. Danegelt was a major cause of the Revolution.

Davanzati: Bernardo Davanzati Bostichi, (1529–1606) of Florence, translator of Tacitus. The imprimaturs are for Davanzati's book *Scisma d'Inghilterra con altre operette* [The Reformation in England and other works], 1638, during Milton's visit to Italy.

Decius: Roman Emperor, ruled 249–251 ce.

ding: Strike heavily, fling.

Diocletian: Roman Emperor, ruled 284–305 ce.

Diodati, Charles: Milton's closest school friend.

Diogenes the Babylonian: The leading Stoic. He was called the Babylonian because he was born at Seleucia.

Diogenes: A Cynic philosopher, believing in the life of the mind, ignoring pleasure and the body.

Dion Prusaeus: The rhetorician Dion Chrysostomos (of the golden lips) was born at Prusa in Bithynia 50 ce. In his 'Ροδιοακος λόγος he scolds the Rhodians for changing inscriptions on old statues.

Dionysius: Plato tutored Dionysios the Elder, Tyrant of Syracuse.

Dionysius Alexandrinus: Bishop of Alexandria (247–265), opponent of the Sabellians.

diffident: Distrustful.

disparagement: Literally, mismatch, misalliance.

dividual: Divisible, separate.

Doric: A Greek mode, used for martial music.

dragon's teeth: On Medea's instructions Jason sowed the teeth of the Colchian dragon, and armed men sprang up.

enchiridion: Handbook, dagger.

encomium: formal high praise

engross: buy large quantities of corn. Engrosser became the modern word grocer, one who buys in quantity.

Epicurus: (342–270 BCE) taught that by virtuous living, one can achieve pleasure, the goal of life. Lucretius describes the ideas of Epicurus in De Rerum Natura.

Epimenides of Crete: (600 BCE). Quoted by Paul in Titus I, 12: "The Cretans are always liars ..." He is rumored to have slept 57 years in a cave.

Epiphanius: Epiphanius (chosen bishop of Salamis in 367) wrote *Panarium* against all heresies.

Epirots: Ἠπειρῶται, persons of Epirus, Asiatics. ἤπειρος mainland.

Erasmus, Desidirius. Dutch humanist, translator of the *New Testament.*

Euripides: Quoted by Paul in I *Corinthians*, XV, 33: "Evil communications corrupt good manners."

Eusebius: (c.264–c.340). Bishop of Caesarea. *A Preparation for the Gospel* by Eusebius (c.264–c.340) is a 15-volume resource that brings together all pagan writings which might be construed as prophecies leading to Christianity.

excremental: Of excrescence, hence superficial.

executioner: one who executes a punishment. Executioners performed branding, nose-slitting, cutting off ears as well as killing.

exorcism: *ἐξορκισμός*—in classical Greek, administering an oath to, binding by oath.

ferula: giant hemlock, used for caning or whipping paddles.

fescue: straw, twig, hence wand or pointer.

fifth essence: After the four elements—earth, air, fire, water—was posited a fifth (*quinta essentia* = fifth essence, hence quintessence) of spirit.

Flaccus: Quintus Horatius Flaccus (Horace) wrote *Satura*, which is usually translated *Satires* but more precisely means social essays in verse.

Flamens: priests attached to certain gods, and later to deified emperors.

fond: Foolish.

Galileo: Galileo Galilei (born 1564), Italian scientist and astronomer, was 74 and recently blind when Milton saw him in 1638. He was in *libera custodia*—no longer confined, but restricted to a villa near Florence.

glossing colors: Flattering pretexts, specious arguments, misrepresentations.

golden rule: Rule of proportion; golden ratio.

Grotius, Hugo: Swedish writer on natural law

Guyon: In Spenser's *Faerie Queene*.

Hall, Bishop: Royalist pamphleteer. Author of *Defence of the Humble Remonstrance* which replies to the Smectymnuus group, to which Milton replied with *Animadversions on the Remonstrant's Defence against Smectymnuus.*

Hannibal: Carthaginian general, who led a campaign of invasion against Rome. Livy (XXVI, ii) reports Hannibal's outrage:

> It was learned from a captive that during those days
> the very ground (as it happened) on which he himself
> was encamped had been sold without any depreciation
> of its value on that account. Now this seemed such
> haughtiness—such insolence—that a buyer should
> have been found at Rome for soil which he himself
> occupied and possessed by right of conquest—that he

immediately summoned an auctioneer and ordered that the money-changers' shops, which then stood about the Roman Forum, should be sold.

Harmony: integrated Bible narratives, diatesseron.

Hercules' pillars: Extent of one's ambitions. The Straits of Gibraltar were said to be the furthest extent of Hercules' travels.

Hercynian wilderness: The mountains along the Danube.

heretics: From Greek αἱρετικός: able to choose, intelligent. αἵρεσις: a choosing; in later Greek, a set of principles.

Homer: Greek epic poet, author of the *Iliad*, the *Odyssey*, and *Homeric Hymns*.

St. Hugh: Parish church in London.

Ianus: archway.

Impeachment: impediment, hindrance.

Independents: Party in Parliament who opposed Presbyterian plans for religion in England; among its leaders was Oliver Cromwell.

Index Expurgatorius: List of books licensed for reading by the Inquisition, begun by Cardinal Caraffa in 1543.

Index Librorum Prohibitorum: Counterpart to *Index Expurgatorius*, this was a Church list of forbidden books.

Inquisition: The Inquisition, or *Sanctum Officium* (Holy Office) was institutionalized by Pope Innocent III to deal with the Albigensian heresies starting in 1198; it spread from France to Italy and Spain, then declined. Ferdinand and Isabella revived it in Spain to crush the Jews and Muslims. The Dominican Thomas de Torquemada was named the first Grand Inquisitor in 1478, with a staff of 200 and a guard of 50 cavalry. Two thousand persons were burned the first year, and many fled from Spain. In 1483 the Pope formally recognized Torquemada. Napoleon abolished it in 1808; in 1814 it was revived and then finally abolished in 1820.

Interlineary: line-by-line translation.

Irenaeus: Only one book of Irenaeus (chosen bishop of Lyons in 177) survives, On Heresies.

Isocrates: author of *Logos Areopagitikos*, the model that Milton used in writing his own *Areopagitica*.

Jan Huss: (1376–1415), Bohemian reformer and follower of Wycliffe, was burned at the stake in 1415.

Janus: The ancient temple of Janus was simply two arches with a chamber between them. The Roman custom during wartime was to keep the doors of Janus' temple open.

St. Jerome: (345–420) Christian editor of the *Vulgate* translation of the Bible, who reported a nightmare in which he is accused of being a Ciceronian, not a Christian, because he read pagan writers.

Jerome of Prague: (1378–1416) Bohemian reformer condemned by the Council of Constance.

Johnson, Samuel: English writer and biographer.

Julian the Apostate: (331–363) Flavius Claudius Julianus. Eastern Roman Emperor, who sought to keep alive Hellenic culture, including polytheism; many saw him as anti-Christian.

Julius Agricola: (37–93). He ruled in Britain from 78 to 85 during the reigns of Vespasian, Titus, and Domitian.

Juno: Roman goddess, the counterpart to the Greek goddess Hera. Out of envy of Alcmena, while she was in labor crying out for her maid, Hera forced the maid to sit cross-legged at the door. Another maid made her think that Alcmena had given birth, and in the moment she uncrossed her legs, Alcmena gave birth to Hercules.

Keri: to be read; rather than edit holy books, rabbinical commentators supplied a correct or more appropriate word in the margin while leaving untouched the word as written in the text (*see chetiv*).

Knox: John Knox, Scots Presbyterian reformer (1515–1572).

Lambeth House: residence of the Archbishop of Canterbury, and one of only two sites designated by the Star Chamber as a licensor of books.

Laud: Archbishop of Canterbury , whose plan was for every bishop to censor every lecturer, as reported in *Articles of Visitation*. Bishop Laud was rumored to wish to become the Patriarch of the Western Church, equal to the Patriarchs of Rome, Jerusalem, Antioch, and Alexandria.

Leo X: John de Medici (Pope 1513–1521) was a patron of letters, a liberal censor of the press but still a censor.

L'Estrange, Roger: English writer who served as official licensor for years.

Limbo: Limbus—fringe, border.

Limbus Fatuorum: Paradise of Fools.

Limbus Infantium: (or Limbus puerorum) for infants who died in original sin.

Limbus Patrum: area for those just persons who had died before Christ.

loosest: Most outspoken.

Loreto: Near Ancona in Italy, Loreto was a pilgrimage site for true believers who wanted to see the very house in which the Virgin Mary was born and lived. It had been transported in 1291 from Palestine to the coast of Dalmatia to Loreto.

Lowell, James Russell: American editor and poet

Lucilius: (148–103 BCE) invented Roman satire.

Lullius: Raymond Lully (1234–1315), medical and chemical writer.

Lucretius: (98–55 BCE) Titus Lucretius Carus, Roman poet. In *De Rerum Natura* he explains Epicurean philosophy, and attacks "religio."

Lycurgus: (ninth century BCE), Spartan lawgiver.

Macaulay, Thomas Babington: English historian.

Malmsey: sweet wine from Malvasia in Morea near Crete.

Malvasia: Greek area where the sweet wine called malmsey is produced.

Mammon: cave of Mammon in Spenser's *Faerie Queene*,

maniples: Company of sixty men in the Roman army.

Margites: Aristotle regards it as the earliest Greek comedy.

Marston Moor: Site of 1644 battle won by forces loyal to Parliament.

St. Martin: Parish church in London.

Martin V: Otto Colonna (ruled as Pope 1417–1431) forbade reading of heretical books, but he did not restrict printing.

Master of his Revels: An official court position in Tudor England.

matrimonial: Until Commonwealth times, people were required to get a marriage license from the Church.

Memmius: C. Memmius Gemellus. He was the patron of Catullus and Cinna; banished in 53 bce for election corruption.

Menander: Greek New Comedy playwright (342–291 bce). Terence imitated Menander.

Mercurius Aulicus: A Royalist periodical (1642–1645) chiefly written by Sir John Birkenhead.

Mercurius Politicus: Parliamentarian periodical, briefly edited by Milton.

Mew: to molt, slough off feathers.

minorites: Franciscan or Grey Friars were called friars minor from the rule of their Order: "Let no one be called prior, but let all be called lesser brethren."

Minos: one of three judges of Hades.

monopoly: exclusive privilege to trade in a commodity; monopolies even of common necessities were greatly abused in the 17th century.

Montemayor, George de: (1520–1562) wrote the popular pastoral romance Diana, which probably influenced Shakespeare's Two Gentlemen of Verona and A Midsummer Night's Dream, as well as Sidney's Arcadia.

More, Thomas: Author of Utopia (meaning "no place," not, as Milton imagined Eutopia, "happy place").

Morgante: Il Morgante Maggiore (1488), a parody by Luigi Pulci (1432–1487) served as the model for Orlando Furioso by Ariosto.

mortal glass: Mirror, as in the magic mirror in medieval times (in Snow White, Chaucer's "Squire's Tale," and cited by Cornelius Agrippa).

mystery: Mystery originally designated guild practices, hence the modern meaning of secrets or trickery.

Naevius: (274 or 264–c.200 bce) Gnaeus Naevius. Epic poet and dramatist.

Naso: Publius Ovidius Naso (Ovid, 43 bce–18 ce) was banished in 9 ce, at age 52, for a book which had been published years before. The real cause was never known.

New Model Army: Reorganization of Parliamentarian forces on the model of Cromwell's brigade, replacing volunteers and mercenaries with dedicated sturdy trained Englishmen.

noble: A noble equalled 6 shillings, 8 pence, or a third of a pound.

obsequies: Acts of worship.

officials: Title of hated officers of Ecclesiastical Courts.

omer: Also called homer, about 0.44 gallon.

Palladian oil: Olive oil; the olive tree was sacred to Pallas Athena, goddess of wisdom.

Pallas Athena: Goddess of wisdom.

Padre Paolo: Pietro Sarpi (1552–1623) took the monastic name Padre Paolo. He was a leading advocate for the Venetian Republic against papal supremacy. His *History of the Council of Trent* was translated into English in 1620 by Nathanael Brent. Milton relies on Sarpi's *Discourse of the Author concerning the Prohibition of Books* for some quotations. The Trentine Council met from 1545 to 1563.

painful: Painstaking.

palace metropolitan: Lambeth Palace.

Paul: The New Testament epistle writer, quotes three Greek poets: Aratos, Euripides, and Epimenides.

Paul III: (1534–1549) started the policy of strict supervision systematized by the Council of Trent. He revived the ancient Dominican Inquisition in a Bull of July 21, 1542.

Paul's: St. Paul's Cathedral, residence of the Bishop of London, and one of two sites chosen by the Star Chamber as licensor of books.

Pembroke, Countess of: Mary Sidney (1561–1621), sister of Sir Philip Sidney, who wrote *Countess of Pembroke's Arcadia*, which she edited after his death and published as *Arcadia* (1590).

Petronius: Petronius Arbiter, Roman satirist, poet of ribaldry (d. 66).

Philemon: (361–263 BCE) New Comedy playwright of Athens. Philemon was a little older than Menander.

Phillips, Edward: biographer of Milton; nephew.

Phillips, John: biographer of Milton; nephew.

Plato: Greek philosopher (428–348 BCE). Plato feared the demoralizing power of poetry and music. In The Republic he banishes fictions which speak ill of the gods or humans, or speak of death.

Plautus: (254–184 BCE) Roman playwright.

pluralist: A person reserving his or her opinion or belonging to more than one party or religion.

Pontifex Maximus: Rome's highest religious post.

Pontific College: Five pontifices (bridge-makers) were engineering mathematicians, who regulated the state calendar for festivals and religious acts.

Pope: Originally all bishops were called Pope, but in 606 Phocas, Emperor of the Eastern Roman Empire, designated it exclusively for the bishop of Rome.

Porphyrius: Neo-Platonist. Porphyry (Malchus or Melech, 233–305 CE) wrote an anti-Christian treatise that was answered by Methodius, Apollinaris, Eusebius, and twenty-five others. Constantine ordered it destroyed.

poundaging: poundage—levies on goods other than wine exported or imported.

pound up: Pen up, as in a village-pound for strayed cattle.

presbyters: Elders. The word, taken from early Christian governing bodies, was used to describe independent Christian communities who did not look to Pope or Archbishop for instructions. This movement was strong in Scotland. In England at this time, Presbyterianism had superseded Episcopalianism (Church of England), and would soon show itself just as intolerant.

Proclus: Neo-Platonist philosopher. Proclus (Diodachos, 412–485 CE) found the Christian view of creation untenable. Neoplatonism was the last serious philosophical rival to Christianity.

professors: Ones who profess pure Christianity, especially Puritans.

Protagoras: (b. 480 BCE), the first Sophist, was born at Abdera in Thrace. He was charged with impiety in 411 bce.

Prynne: (1600–1669) Puritan who attacked Arminianism and stage plays. By Star Chamber decrees in 1634 and 1637 he lost his ears and was branded. When Parliament took control, he was in the forefront, attacking Laud, but also opposing one of Milton's pamphlets, opposing the Presbyterians. He favored a new state-organized church.

Psyche: In an episode of *The Golden Ass* of Apuleius, Venus is angry at Psyche's falling in love with her son, and sets her an impossible task of separating seeds. An army of ants perform the work for Psyche before nightfall.

Pulci: Luigi Pulci (1432–1487) wrote *Il Morgante Maggiore* (1488), a parody that served as the model for *Orlando Furioso* by Ariosto.

puny: From puis-né, post-natus, afterborn.

Puritans: Name for the generally middle of the road partisans who wanted to purify English religion of the Roman hierarchy.

Pym: (1584–1643) Leader in the Short Parliament which was dissolved, he then petitioned for a new Parliament, and that won he led the fight to impeach Strafford, the King's chief minister, and Archbishop Laud.

Pyrrhus: (318–272 BCE). Fought against the Romans 280–275 bce.

Quadragesimal: to be excused from fasting at Lent

Quadrivium: Medieval sciences of arithmetic, geometry, astronomy, and music

Read, Herbert: English critic

rebeck: A three-stringed violin-like instrument, played with a bow.

refutations of merchandise: Tricks of trade.

Rhadamanth: The three judges of Hades were Rhadamanth, Minos and Aiakos.

Richardson, J.: Editor and biographer of Milton

Richelieu: Minister to Louis XIII 1624–1642, worked to make the French monarchy absolute.

Root and branch party: Radical party in Parliament who voted for immediate drastic measures.

Roundel: round, ring dance.

Roundheads: The Parliamentary army, many of whom wore relatively short hair. The name came from a Royalist princess, who asked about Pym, "Who is that round-headed man?"

Sarpi, Pietro: (1552–1623) Venetian patriot. See Padre Paolo.

Scipio: (185–129 BCE) Scipio the Younger, the conqueror of Carthage. Cicero used him as the chief spokesperson in his De Republica.

Scotus: John Duns Scotus (c.1265–1308).

Mr. Selden: John Selden (1584–1654), legal writer, forced to recant one book, the *History of Tithes* (1618). Milton praised Selden's *On Natural Law and the Law of Nations, according to the system of the Hebrews*: "a work more useful and more worthy to be perused by whosoever studies to be a great man in wisdom, equity, and justice than all those 'decretals and sumless sums' which the pontifical clerks have doted on."

Seville: The seat of the Spanish Inquisition was Seville.

Sir Philip Sidney: (1554–1586) English poet and soldier. Sidney was member of an Areopagus Society, dedicated to bring classical meters into English verse. Author of *Arcadia* (1590).

Sixtus IV: (1417–1431) forbade printing heretical books.

Skelton: Possibly Henry VIII's "Vicar of Hell," actually a Rector of Diss in Norfolk.

Socrates: Here, Socrates Scholasticus of Constantinople (379–450?), who wrote a history of the early Christian Church.

sol-fa: From the hymn *Sol facit*, coined by Guido Aretino (1020?) to designate two notes of the do-re-mi scale.

sophisms: Tricks of trade.

Sophron Mimus: Sophron (fl. 460–420 BCE) wrote mime plays. Scaliger defines a *mime* as a poem imitating any action to stir up laughter.

Sorbonne: The school founded by Robert de Sorbon in 1252 in Paris. This ecclesiastical college was influential in French Catholicism; it was rebuilt by Richelieu in 1619, and finally dissolved in 1789.

spill: Destroy.

sponge: Spunge or expunge, erase from a Roman wax tablet.

standards: weights and measures.

Star Chamber: high court of justices, with no recourse

Stationers' Company: Guild of printers in England

statists: Statesmen or stateswomen.

statutes: securities given for debts contracted

Strafford, Thomas Wentworth: (1593–1641) English statesman. He established strong government measures in Ireland to calm the troubles of English settlement there, but then used the same methods in England as Charles I's chief minister.

Sublimate: to vaporize a solid.

suburb trenches: Milton's eighth sonnet was sparked by a November 1642 confrontation of Royalist and Parliamentary forces at Brentford and Turnham Green, suburbs of London, that led to no battle. In 1643, twelve miles of "suburb trenches" were dug by volunteer labor, for London had no natural defenses.

success: Outcome, not necessarily good.

Suetonius: Roman historian.

Synopsis: overview.

syntagma: Summary, general handbook.

Thales: Thaletas of Crete, musician and poet, not to be confused with Thales of Miletus, the philosopher. However, this is a doubtful story: Thaletas lived a hundred years later than Lycurgus.

St. Thomas: Parish church in London.

Thorough: Plan of Strafford's to put everything in England under monarchic control. See p. 17.

Tickets: credit chits

Titus Livius: (59 BCE–17 CE) Known as Livy. This portion of Livy's *Histories* is lost, but Tacitus reports: "Titus Livius, eminently distinguished for eloquence and for honesty, praised Pompey so highly that Augustus called him a Pompeian; but that did not hurt their friendship."

Toland, John: biographer of Milton.

tonnage: Tunnage—levies or customs on wine.

topic folio: Greek τόποι—common places, hence commonplace book.

Transylvanian: The custom has been verified from enrollment records at universities. Transylvania was staunchly Protestant during the Thirty Years' War. Perhaps the "Transylvanian" was Samuel Hartlib, Milton's friend, who had been born in Poland.

Hartlib also invited John Amos Comenius of Moravia to visit London 1641–1642.

Trent: Council of Trent or Trentine Council met from 1545 to 1563, issuing increasingly severe edicts.

triennial parliament: After Charles I dissolved Parliament in 1629, eleven years passed without a sitting Parliament. The Triennial Act, passed in 1641, called for sessions every three years whether or not officially assembled.

triple ice: Aes triplex, in Horace's *Odes*, I, 3, 9.

Trivium: Medieval sciences of grammar, logic, and rhetoric.

trophy: monument.

Turkish Empire: Printing was not allowed in Turkey until the mid-eighteenth century.

Twelve Tables: The Ten Tables was the first and only legal code of Rome, prepared by the Decemvirs in 451 bce, later supplemented by two more. A Roman father from earliest times had unlimited power over his children, including murder, a law confirmed in the law of the Twelve Tables. Although it fell into disfavor and disuse in the later Republic, this law was not struck down until 318 ce.

Tyrtaeus: Greek poet born in Attica but lived in Sparta.

Utopian: referring to *Utopia* by Sir Thomas More. Milton's spelling was Eutopia (happy place), a misreading of More's intention for Utopia (no place).

Verres: Propraetor in Sicily 73–71 bce. He was an extortionist, against whom Cicero composed seven Verrine Orations.

Vetus Comoedia: Old Comedy of Athens (458–404 bce) of broad personal political satire: by Kratinos, Eupolis, Aristophanes. This was succeeded by Middle Comedy (404–338 bce) of general satire, and New Comedy (338–260 bce) social comedy of manners.

Viscount St. Albans: See Francis Bacon.

vulgar tongue: National language derived from Latin.

Westminster Chapel: A convocation, or national assembling of clergy, was called by the Long Parliament in July 1643 at the Westminster Assembly

Williams, Raymond: critic and historian

Wood, Anthony à: biographer of Milton.

Wyclif: Wycliffe (1324?–1384) decried churchly abuses and translated the *Bible* into English. The Council of Constance (1414–1418) ordered Wycliffe's bones to be dug up and burned.

Young, Thomas: Private tutor to Milton, a Scotsman.

Zenger, John Peter: (1697–1746) Zenger published the *New York Weekly*, a partisan paper opposed to colonial governor William Cosby. After a year of abuse, Cosby had him arrested. Andrew Hamilton, his lawyer, argued that the jury, not the judge, should decide not only whether the material in question had been published, but also whether it was libellous.

Zwinglius: Ulrich Zwingli (1484–1531), Reformation leader.